GAUDI GUID

Editorial Gustavo Gili, S.A.

08029 Barcelona   Rosselló, 87-89
Spain
Tel. (343) 322 81 61   Fax (343) 322 92 05

Xavier Güell

GG

Translation: Graham Thomson
Cover design: Eulàlia Coma

1st edition 1991
2nd edition 1994

ISBN: 84-252-1558-7
Depósito legal: B.13.479-1994
Printed in Spain by INGOPRINT, S.A. - Barcelona

Index

Acknowledgements

The preparation of this book was made possible thanks to the material and assistance provided by the following:

José Antonio Martínez Lapeña
Elías Torres
Carles Fochs
Pedro Uhart
Toshiaki Tange
Raquel Lacuesta
Antoni González
Eugeni Bofill
Francesc Morera
Eduard Bru
Jaume Duró
Marta Fernández de la Reguera
The review *D'A*
Neus Moyano
Lluís Casals
Lluís M.ª Güell Cortina

ANTONI GAUDÍ I CORNET WAS BORN IN Reus, Tarragona, on the 25th of June 1852. He attended the College of the Padres Escolapios in Reus and then studied architecture at the Escuela Provincial de Arquitectura de Barcelona, where he was awarded the diploma on the 15th of March, 1878. While still studying architecture, Gaudí also worked in the studio of the architect Josep Fontseré, from 1877 until 1882. With Fontseré he worked on the design of details for one of the most important projects then being undertaken in Barcelona: the Parc de la Ciutadella. Gaudí is believed to have contributed to the design of the main gates of this impressive park.

In 1878, in response to a public competition, he designed and manufactured lampposts for the Plaça Reial in Barcelona. These early examples of his work, still to be seen in their original locations, mark the beginnings of Gaudí's connection with Barcelona, the city which was to provide the geographical setting for virtually all his subsequent activity, and where he was to carry out his most important work.

Between 1883 and 1926, Gaudí constructed ten schemes of quite different kinds in Barcelona, ranging from private houses to schools, from apartment building in the Eixample, pavilions, and an estate planned as a garden-city, to the Temple of the Sagrada Familia.

I woluld like to make special mention of this last piece of work, for a number of reasons. The principal, and perhaps the most attractive reason, is this: few architects nowadays have the chance to explain their work in two quite distinct modes; one being to follow their work in chronological sequence (the most usual way), the other being to follow the development of that work through the evolution of a single project —the Expiatory Temple of the Sagrada Familia. There can be no doubting the importance of understanding the evolution of this construction in parallel with the other buildings Gaudí worked on in his different periods. The evolution of Gaudí's architecture, which is clearly reflected in the sequence of projects he produced, has to be understood as a constant effort to discover new solutions, based on the progress

Previous pages: armchairs for the Palau Güell

Gaudí aged 36. The photograph from his exhibitor's pass for the Barcelona Universal Exposition of 1888

achieved in the carrying out of the project immediatelly before.

From 1883 to 1890, Gaudí was occupied on the completion of the crypt for the Sagrada Familia and, in parallel with this, working on the construction of the Vicens house, the Capricho in Comillas, the pavilions on the Güell estate and the Palau Güell. This period can be seen as being marked by the relationship between the different styles and, above all, the eclecticism of Gaudí's approach.

Between 1891 and 1990, Gaudí built the apse and began the Nativity facade, which asks to be read in parallel with the construction of the Episcopal Palace in Astorga, the Theresan Convent, the Fernández Andrés house in León and the Calvet house. This was a period characterised by its rootedness in Neogothicism, which undoubtedly served as a point of departure, although Gaudí did not forget to «make a commitment to absolute sincerity», a phrase coined by the architect and teacher Eugène Emmanuel Viollet-le-Duc (1814-1879).

From 1901 to 1926, Gaudí devoted himself to the construction of the Nativity facade and, from 1903 on, to the raising of the four bell towers, which ought to be read in the context of this most fruitful period of his life, the period which earned him international recognition and prestige as an architect: the Torre Bellesguard house, Park Güell, the wall and gate for the Miralles estate, the restoration of the Cathedral in Palma de Mallorca, the Batlló house, the Milà house, the crypt for the Colonia Güell and the Sagrada Familia schoolrooms. These years at the start of the new century were marked by work which is quite exceptional, individual, assured and daring. This taking of risks is of particular importance, and should be seen as something antisocial, and the main factor in the isolation and incomprehension which accompanied the last ten years of his working life, obstinately devoted to the realisation of a utopia.

Unquestionably, this parallel reading will be borne in mind by the reader of the present guide, without neglecting the unitary character possessed by the Temple of the Sagrada Familia in its own right.

The sheer volume and density of the commissions which constitute Gaudí's work allow us to divide it up, in this introduction, into a series of aspects which it would be useful to treat in isolation. These aspects range from the more general vision embodied in urban design through to those qualities which are rather to be found in Gaudí's detailing and his work as a designer. To put it another way, this vision corresponds to the process which runs from the first sketch designs for each project, which clearly pertain exclusively to Gaudí's own ratiocination, to the work undertaken together with his numerous team of assistants in the final stage of each one of his schemes.

There is a homogeneity to Gaudí's way of carrying out all of his schemes; from the first ideas as to how to situate a building in a given context, whether this be clearly defined or devoid of any system of coordinates, through to the most minute ornamental details, on the facade or in some corner of the interior. The first examples of Gaudí's work for us to look at are the Vicens house and the Temple of the Sagrada Familia. The Vicens house is of interest as an example of Gaudí's early work, showing how he approached the siting of his building in the network of narrow streets which make up the urban fabric of the Gràcia district. Gaudí sets his house against the party wall to the east, enjoying the view to the south offered by carrer Aulèstia i Pijoan, in order to obtain two contrasting vistas, one urban and consolidated, the other, more ludic, looking out over the garden where he was to construct two noteworthy elements: a compact, cylindrical gazebo with a dome and a spire on its west side, and a free-standing volume which uses a fountain as its pretext, very similar to the arch still to be seen in the environs of the Faculty of Pharmacology, and which belonged to the Güell family. We can see, then, how the siting of the house avoids giving direct access from the street and how, by means of little backward movements, a unified conception merges the palm leaf fence with the facade of the house. The urban design for the Temple of the Sagrada Familia belongs to a different order and another context, yet the two pieces of work are contemporary.

The layout of the Temple, in accordance with the principles of the Pla Cerdà plan for

Views of the railings enclosing the Ciutadella park, lampposts in the Plaça Reial and interior and exterior views of the Vicens house

Optimal visibility study for the Temple of the Sagrada Familia, volumetric axonometric sketch of the Palau Güell and transverse section of the Temple of the Sagrada Familia

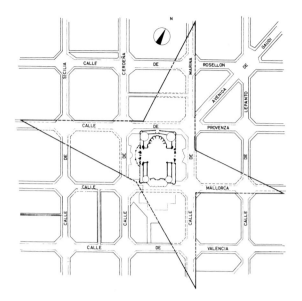

Barcelona's expansion, is absolutely Cartesian, although mitigated by its proportions. Gaudí occupies the entire space of the north-south axis with the building's floor plan, neglecting to allow for the main access to the Temple. His recourse to a great flight of steps leading up to the House of God is nonetheless valid, while he uses the large landing, with its two levels, in front of the three doors to resolve the conflict between the vehicular traffic on carrer Mallorca and pedestrian access to the Temple. Gaudí does not, however, find a pragmatic solution for something as important as the frontal view of the main facade, with its necessarily stepped plinth. The study of optimum visibility for the Temple reveals the complex fragmentation of these sightlines. I would only add that, thanks to the «Latin cross» layout, the dimensions of the Temple's east-west axis fit perfectly into the dimensions of the city block. The question of whether the main facade ought to look south rather than west belongs to a different order of consideration, and the present text is not the appropriate place to debate it.

As we have already noted, Gaudí's work allows two quite separate readings. One would consist in the analysis of all his schemes, from 1880 to 1926, in chronological sequence, and the other would focus on a single building: the Temple of the Sagrada Familia (1883-1926). It is for this reason that a parallel examination of the two lines of development is of particular interest, in that it allows us to perceive the overlaps and interconnections between the Sagrada Familia and Gaudí's other works. The interest of this approach lies in the fact that there are a number of quite evident points of contact, and at the same time certain contradictions. In any case, Gaudí's work is perhaps exemplary in that it can be assessed in a fragmentary fashion, project by project, as well as, exceptionally read through the Temple of the Sagrada Familia.

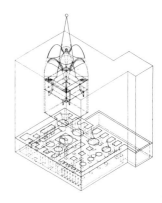

The next scheme to be discussed is the Palau Güell (1886-1889), and more specifically the view through the section along an axis which bisects the volume of the main salon. Gaudí situates this main salon at the geometrical centre of the Palau. In so doing he resolves a whole series of questions ranging from the reading which regards the salon as an element to be assimilated to the central courtyard, with different rooms on different levels opening onto it, to more intimate considerations such as the distancing of the principal space from the two facades: the main facade and its opposite. This salon, which can be used as a place to walk around or through, or to pray in, since it contains a concealed altar behind elaborate, richly ornamented doors, is the essential core of the building. Nevertheless, in the interior of the salon we are aware only of the shifting incidence of the light, as in a temple: in other words, we perceive the sun's movement through the openings in the roof vault, or thanks to the chiaroscuro of the rose windows, through which the sun's rays are filtered as in the depths of a forest. This symbiosis between religious space and occult space, characteristic of the period, can be seen as analogous to the central dome of the Temple of the Sagrada Familia, a very high cupola (170 metres) which Gaudí, engaged at the time in building the Palau, must have seen as an ideal.

A diametrically opposed position to this might be formulated with regard to the building for the Theresan religious order (1888-1890). It would be out of place to impose parallel readings appraising the rigorous construction of the Theresan building, which is the embodiment of a controlled, austere design, in relation to the formal conception of the Temple which presents itself to us as being full of variants in form and construction. If we compare the plans of the two buildings, we can see that, in the first, Gaudí resorts to the use of a small hypostile chamber at the east and west extremes of the floors occupied by bedrooms. These spaces, which should be understood as «beginning and end» of the corridor, are fed by a light which enters longitudinally through the two courtyards. The sense of an elongated cloister thus created is best appreciated on the first floor, as the courtyard which the upper floors overlook is larger and the corridor which links together the various adjoining rooms lacks the beauty of proportion to be found on the first floor.

In Gaudí's project for the Temple, the conception and location of the cloister is innovative. From being merely a kind of annexe, square in plan, with a single point of connection with the central nave of the church, it has become an element which runs the full length of the building's perimeter. This conception of the cloister-cum-quayside, absorbing and regulating the Temple's capacity to insulate its interior from the bustle of the city, is quite disconcerting when compared with the model of the cloister we considered above. This is a bold, even disturbing conception of the cloister, to be understood as an innovation in its approach to religion and architecture.

This similarity between enclosed longitudinal cloister and open perimeter explains the place and the functional relationship which must exist in every community, whether closed or open to the city.

Very nearly following chronological sequence, the next piece of work for us to consider is the Calvet house (1898-1904). This scheme coincides with an important period in the construction of the Temple. Gaudí, when he started to develop his conception of the bell towers, thought that these should be square in plan and rotated through forty-five degrees, in such a way that the arris would lighten the excessively heavy Nativity facade. Just as the work of constructing the two pairs of free-standing towers was about to go ahead, he saw the need to change the geometry, moving to a new, circular order. Obviously the inscription of two circles inside two squares was going to leave the corners exposed. Gaudí resolved this discrepancy with the incorporation of an element which can be understood as a kind of viewing gallery or balcony. If we consider the texture of the stonework on the Calvet house and compare it with that of the towers, we can see that they are virtually the same.

On the facade of the Calvet house, and in contrast to what other architects of the time were doing on houses with a programme of this type, Gaudí has placed a single, enclosed, angular balcony precisely on the entrance axis, serving only the main floor of the house. The rest of the facade is given over to the window openings corresponding to the bedrooms on the different floors, with their wrought iron balustrades, all of the same dimensions. This detail, far from usual in the residential buildings of the Eixample, serves to cast greater emphasis on the one element which projects out from the facade. It is curious to note the similarity between a viewing gallery, the outcome of an exercise in geometry, and this single balcony, both of reduced dimensions.

In 1906, Gaudí accepted the commission to build the Milà i Camps house, better known as «La Pedrera» —«the stone quarry». The dimensions of the plot, with three facades, were grand enough for it to be apparent that this building could be approached as two separate units. This prompted the creation of

The enclosed balcony of the Calvet house, views of the circular courtyard of the Milà house and interior views of the towers of the Temple of the Sagrada Familia

two courtyards, one completely circular, on the «xamfrà» or chamfered corner of carrer Provença and the passeig de Gràcia, and a second courtyard, also with rounded ends, but oblong, aligned with carrer Provença. At this point we must return once more to the Temple of the Sagrada Familia to recall the plan of one of the bell towers and consider it alongside the plan of this circular courtyard. The similarity between the two plans is evident. The first, consisting of two concentric rings and an interior staircase, develops upwards as a helix. The second, a single ring, is composed of a series of pillars which, without ceasing to be circular, successively approach the limits of the facade and the adjoining walls. This undoubtedly structural concept has a profound influence on the construction of «La Pedrera».

If we recall the tambour, with its twelve cylindrical columns, which explains the change in geometry we have already remarked in the plan of the towers, we can see it as being the true support for the bell towers. If we consider the interior aspect of the bell towers as they rise upwards, and then do the same with the circular courtyard of the Milà house, as we look up we can appreciate the great similarity between these two interiors with their highly accentuated verticality.

Let us now look at the way the exterior of the towers has been handled, and compare it with the facade of «La Pedrera». If we focus our attention on the block of stone whose slanting position serves to direct the sound of the bells above downwards to the neighbourhood below, we observe that this strongly resembles the profile and section of

Views of the roof spaces of the Torre Bellesguard house and the Milà house

the facade of «La Pedrera», immediately recognising the similarity between this inclined piece of stone and the little windows around the roof space.

If we continue to search out analogies, we might consider another point of coincidence. If we take a portion of bell tower and open it up longitudinally, we obtain a plane surface. When we superimpose this onto the facade of «La Pedrera» we find that both have the same number of openings and, by extension, the same number of circular columns —twelve— supporting this facade. Of course, this process has to be applied to each of the courtyards, and if we then put the two together we find that we have the plan which, spread out like a sheet, forms the three faces of this facade. We might add a further detail: the facade of the Milà house is constructed of a single material which makes up the three sides of the Cerdà block, with the subtle assistance of Josep Maria Jujol's wrought iron balustrades. In 1910, Gaudí completed this house while, at the same time, the bell towers of the Temple continued their slow ascent. This was to be the last wholly new building which Gaudí was to carry through to completion.

It was not until 1908, after ten years of studies and tests, that construction began on the chapel commissioned by Eusebi Güell for his new textiles factory in Santa Coloma de Cervelló.

In this proyect we can see how Gaudí, once more, makes full use of the opportunity to further his studies of construction and structures. The experience afforded him by the progress of construction work on the Temple of the Sagrada Familia had revealed to him the need to modify certain elements. Gaudí was evidently dissatisfied with the formal outcome of the crypt of the Temple, even after he had made a number of slight changes to the project by Villar y Lozano. As a result, he took a significant step forward in the structural design of this new chapel, saving on unnecessary effort and employing formal abstraction once again as a means of developing his conception of space.

We are fortunate in having a couple of Gaudí's own sketches to show us the exterior configuration of the chapel. In these we can see a combination of features which, without forgetting the Temple of the Sagrada Familia, direct us back to the Milà house.

I would like to conclude this introduction by drawing the attention of the person intending to use this guide to two interior spaces. The first is the roof space of the Milà house where, before it was adapted for use as an attic apartment, it was possible to appreciate the construction of a series of parabolic arches with the handmade bricks laid in only two stretcher-bonded courses; the second is the interior space of the crypt; in both, the light penetrates from the side; in both, the arches are held together by the continuous thread of the key course; in both, the same precedent is apparent, the attic floor of the Bellesguard house.

Work built
in Barcelona

Vicens house
1883-1888

C/ Carolines, 18-24

VISITING: Private residence.

TRANSPORT: Buses 16, 17, 22, 24, 28; Metro L3 (Fontana); FF.CC. Generalitat (Gràcia).

POSITION ON THE PLAN: **1**

THIS SUMMER HOUSE FOR THE CERAMICS manufacturer Manuel Vicens Muntaner was the first scheme to be built by Gaudí as an architect. Dating from the end of the 19th century, this building paved the way for the introduction of contemporary currents in European architecture into Catalonia, currents which were to promote a new architecture.

Clearly oriental in inspiration, rooted in Arabic and Mudejar architecture, the use this project makes of decorative ceramics is remarkable: there are only two patterns of tile featured on the facades, cladding this unusual building, unique in the context of the Gràcia district of Barcelona. This cladding envelops the two main storeys of the building - ground and first floor - in horizontal bands, while the attic and roof space is treated with vertical lines which double on the upper space. The formal and mutually compensatory interplay of these two treatments, in their various applications, is clearly concerned with juxtaposition, giving the house a powerful compactness. Of interest, too, are the railings which enclose the house and set it apart from the street. The property has an extensive garden which runs as far back as avinguda Princep d'Asturies, with a number of different elements such as a large fountain, raised terraces and a pavilion in one corner, all of which offer a variety of views of this, Gaudí's first piece of work in his own right. A section of the railings (palmetto leaves) which once enclosed the garden is now to be found at the main entrance to the Park Güell, on carrer Olot.

The house was extended, in 1925, by the architect Serra Martínez, who virtually doubled the original volume, while closely followng the house's stylistic criteria and preserving its unity.

Inevitably, as this is a private residence, its interiors - drawing rooms, dining room, smoking room and so on - can only be studied by consulting photographs.

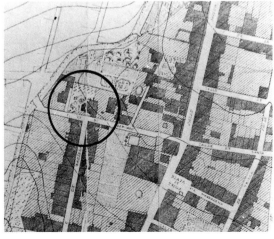

General view of the house
and site plan for the project

Plan and elevation of the
project and plan of the ground
floor in its present state.
Elevation of the carrer
Carolines facade, drawn by
Enric Serra Grau

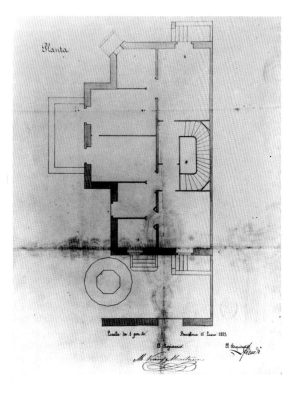

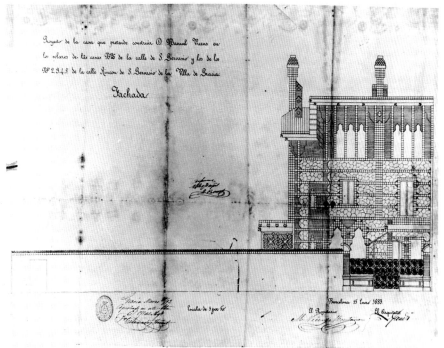

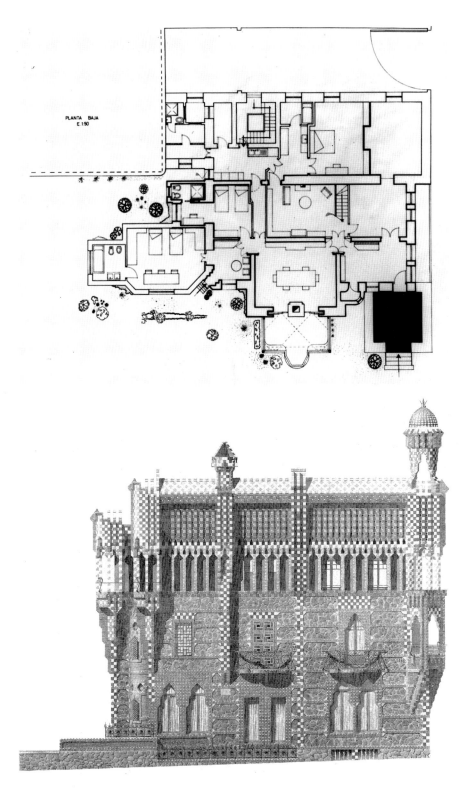

PLANTA BAJA
E 1:50

25

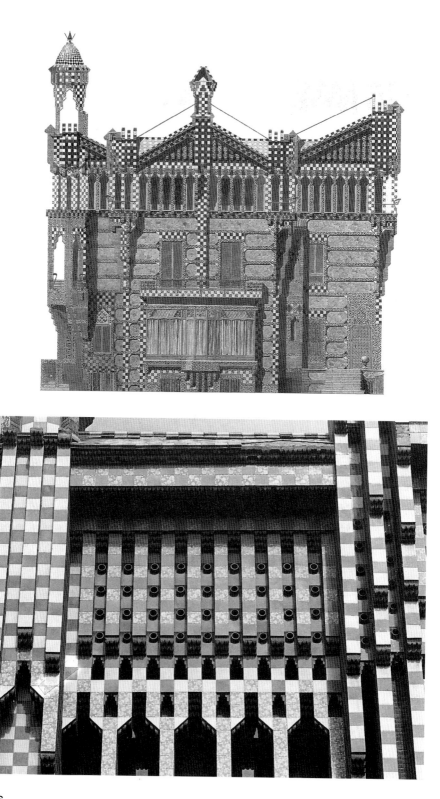

Elevation of the garden
facade, drawn by Fco. Javier
Saura Manich. Partial and
general views of the house
before extension in 1925

Following pages: two details
of the facade

Various views of the interior
and details of the railings and
the bars over the windows

Pavilions in the Güell estate

1884-1887

Avinguda de Pedralbes, 7

VISITING: Occupied by the Càtedra Gaudí, open to the public during term-time.

TRANSPORT: Buses 7, 22, 64; Metro L3 (Palau).

POSITION ON THE PLAN: 2

THIS SMALL CONSTRUCTION, LOCATED in the residential district of Barcelona, should be understood as a pair of pavilions linked by a grand gate which gives access to an estate used by the Güell family for recreational purposes.

If we study the layout of these two pavilions, which seek to perfectly accomplish their function of enclosing the estate, we notice the passage from massive walls to a sloping and almost transparent plane which allows a view of the garden adjacent to the two pavilions: one the gatekeeper's lodge, the other, and larger, a coach-house and stable for horses. The gatekeeper's lodge, which stands to the left of the grand entrance to the estate, is composed of one space with an octagonal plan, covered by a cupola and crowned by a spire, and another, rectangular space, both with the same stylistic character. The stables, to the right, abut on the turret which supports the great iron gate with the figure of a dragon. This latter element, its design calculated to intimidate the visitor, effectively gives dynamism and tension to the relationship between the two pavilions, its wrought iron worked in a variety of different treatments. The whole composed by this gate and the side door for pedestrians quite clearly indicates the tremendous effort which Gaudí was to consistently devote to the design of "auxiliary" elements on a day-to-day basis in most of his schemes. The pavilion built as stables, which currently houses the Càtedra Gaudí, consists of two elements: a first volume, with a small vestibule and staircase leading up to the roof, and a second, larger area, rectangular in plan, in which the parabolic vaults and arches are the architectural elements which support and roof the interior space. Of importance here is the lighting: the quality of the light which enters through the trapezoidal upper openings between the vaults encourages the visitor to perceive a certain monastic air here.

Plans, elevations and
perspective, drawn by Ricard
A. Vicente

Following pages: views of the
two pavilions and the gate
seen from the interior

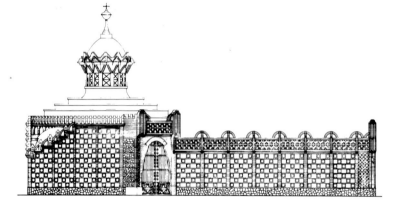

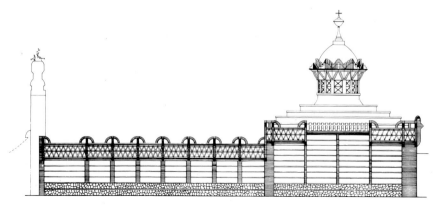

Various details of the pavilions

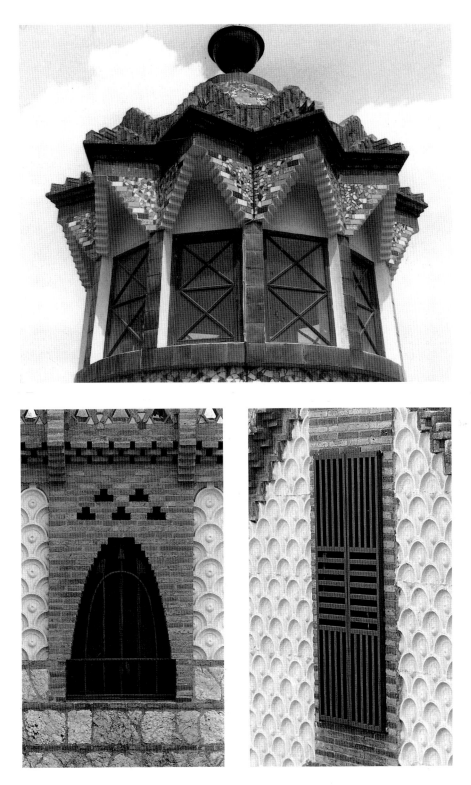

39

Axonometric sketch by
Roberto Pane; transverse and
longitudinal sections, view of
the interior and details of the
exterior

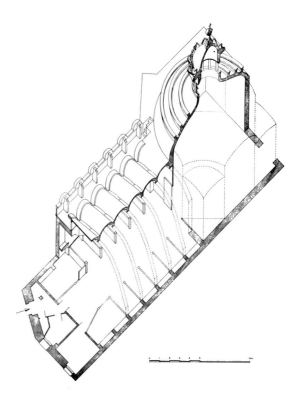

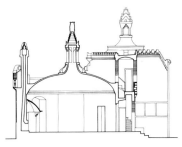

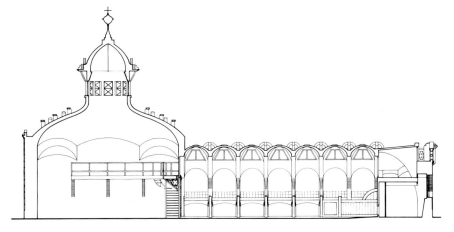

41

Palau Güell

1886-1889

C/ Nou de la Rambla, 9

VISITING: Tuesday to Saturday from 11.00 to 14.00 and from 16.00 to 19.00. Special visits by arrangement with the Servei de Patrimoni Arquitectònic (Diputació de Barcelona), tel. 402 21 73.

TRANSPORT: Buses 14, 18, 38, 59; Metro L3 (Liceu).

POSITION ON THE PLAN: 3

THE CONSTRUCTION OF THIS NEW Barcelona residence for Eusebi Güell i Bacigalupi, industrialist, intellectual, great patron of the arts in general and of Gaudí in particular, coincided with one of the most splendid moments in the city's history: the preparations for the Universal Exposition of 1888.

Alongside its specific function as a family house, the new residence was intended to accomodate some of the grandest social events of its day, as well as cultural evenings and colloquies. Gaudí carried out numerous studies for the treatment of the main facade, of which he presented only two for Güell to choose from, his client deciding on the project which Gaudí himself preferred. A visit to this town house, now the property of the Diputació de Barcelona, should be conducted with some care, since each floor is of quite exceptional interest.

The basement floor, with its great cylindrical pillars of handmade brick, crowned by wide conical capitals, was occupied by the stables, with access by way of a spiral ramp leading down from ground level. On the ground floor, the two arches which unmistakably signal the main access to the *palau*, designed to accomodate the carriages of the time, conduct the visitor in to the flight of stairs which, by way of a mezzanine, proceeds up to the *piano nobile* of the building. This is exclusively given over to the various drawing rooms and salons in which receptions were to be held. The large main salon, an absolutely unique space, stands at the geometrical centre under the cupola, just as the dome would do in the transept of an ecclesiastical floor plan; richly and complexly constructed, this cupola has small circular openings which dimly illuminate the space.

The upper floor, following the approved functional order, is occupied by bedrooms. However, there is a mezzanine just beneath this dormitory floor where Güell had his office, connected with the main salon by way of a balcony.

The top floor, designed for the servants' rooms, is relatively interesting in terms of the slight value usually invested in this kind of space.

The main facade is clad in marble on its lower floors in the manner of a plinth, giving a grander, more palatial and urbane quality to the finish. This is followed by masonry cladding, more historicist in style, which composes the different floors and the rear facade. The entrance, which we mentioned above, is perfectly symmetrical, and is indicated by the openings of the two parabolic archways. The positioning of these openings, and the grand gallery which runs almost the whole length of the facade, as well as the parapet with its discreet little stepped crenellations which complement the chimneys, and the ventilation shafts, no two the same, together compose this perfectly rhythmic plane, in a tone between grey and white, which recalls Venetian Gothic.

The rear facade, which looks south, boasts one highly unusual element, which projects out from the stone plane of the facade: a gallery with rounded ends under a balcony and pergola. This composite feature is like a large screen, coming down to shelter the back of the house from the heat of the summer sun.

The interior of the palau has been treated with an exceptional wealth of detail. Wooden panelling, marble columns, marquetry work and specially designed furniture give every room of the house a quality of its own, quite different from the rest. Attentiveness to every detail, and the ability to appreciate the efforts made by Gaudí and his co-workers are indispensable prerequisites for a visit to the Palau Güell.

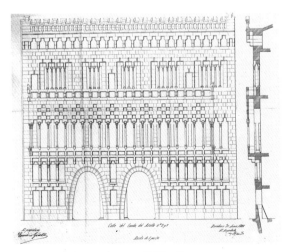

Study for the elevation of the main facade in 1886

Sectional axonometric sketch
by the Amigos de Gaudí and
elevation of the main facade,
drawn by Rosa Cortés Pagés

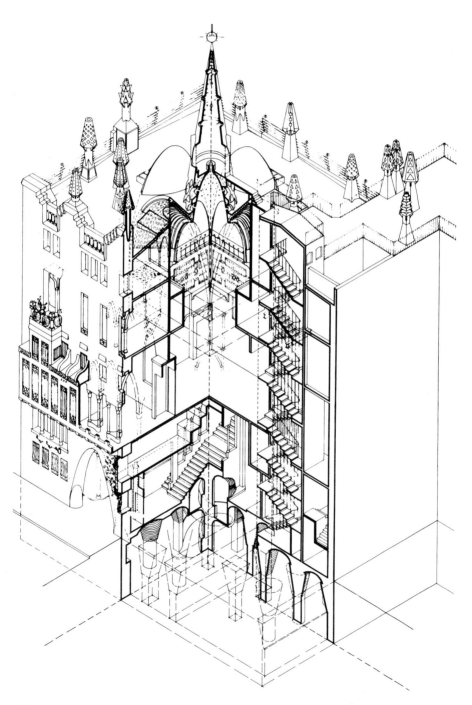

Following pages: transverse section and details of the covered gallery and sunshade on the rear facade

Detail and interior view of the cupola over the main drawing room and part of the transverse section drawn by Antoni Ortiz López

Section and detail of the arches and pillars of the gallery on the rear facade and detail of the capitals of the pillars in the *piano nobile* by the main facade

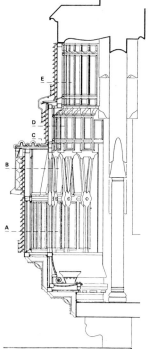

Interior view of one of the
entrance gates and plan,
elevations and general view of
the dressing table

Following pages: view of the
main drawing room

Theresan convent

1888-1890

C/ de Ganduxer, 85-105

VISITING: Permission to view the interior can be requested from the nun at the door.

TRANSPORT: Buses 14, 16; FF. CC. Generalitat (Les Tres Torres).

POSITION ON THE PLAN: **4**

THIS FREE-STANDING BUILDING, rectangular in plan (approximately 58 × 18 metres) was designed from the outset exclusively as an educational establishment. Regarded as a whole, it might at first seem to resemble an industrial building, both with regard to the materials employed and the repetition of the window module in the frontal composition of the four facades.

There are certain aspects of this building which it is important to appreciate. If we study the main facade attentively, to focus on the most immediate feature, we can see that the height of the windows, framed within perfectly fashioned parabolic arches, varies according to whether they are on the ground floor, first, second or third floor. Just as in the buildings of the Eixample, the proportions of the openings vary in order to communicate the greater importance of the lower as compared with the upper floors.

Gaudí's treatment of the functional programme has located the classrooms and related rooms on ground and first floors, while the second and third floors are taken up by dormitories for boarding pupils.

Another feature which relates to the most interesting interior spaces is to be seen in the corridors on the ground and first floors. Here a perfectly centred corridor runs from one end of the building to the other, giving access to the various rooms. On the floor above, this space is doubled. The formerly single corridor unfolds, opens out, with the appearance of lightwells which illuminate this new circulation route. This coming and going along different corridors makes for an internal circulation which ought to be understood as recalling the monastery cloisters of mediaeval architecture. These routes are constituted by, once again, parabolic arches, with the aim of creating a space that is quiet, secluded and more suitably proportioned for the practices of meditation and prayer associated with the place.

Returning to the facades, it is worth fixing our attention on the little turrets set exactly on the four corners, each crowned by the four-armed ceramic cross, a characteristic element in Gaudí's architecture.

Finally, it should be pointed out that this building, which was constructed at a modest

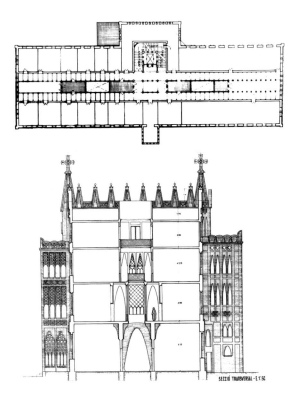

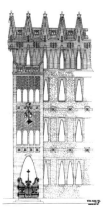

Typical floor plan drawn by Lluís Bonet; transverse section, detail of the main facade and general view of the rear facade

SECCIÓ TRANSVERSAL - E.1:50

Period photograph of a classroom and details of the wrought iron entrance gate, the cross which crowns the corner, the corridor and the construction of a window opening

cost, is imbued with an atmosphere of austerity and rationalism not often found in Gaudí's work, yet which here perfectly satisfy the programme and the internal content.

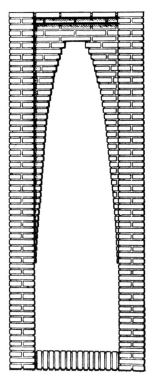

Calvet house
1898-1904

C/ Casp, 48

VISITING: Private apartment building; the entrance hall can be visited.

TRANSPORT: Buses 7, 18, 19, 22, 24, 35, 39, 41, 42, 45, 47, 55, 56, 58; Metro L1, L4 (Urquinaona).

POSITION ON THE PLAN: **5**

THIS IS THE FIRST EXAMPLE IN GAUDÍ'S work of a rented apartment building on a gap site, constructed in the Eixample for the family of the textile manufacturer Pedro Calvet.

Although outwardly very similar in appearance to other buildings in this part of the Eixample, a visit to the building's entrance hall will reveal a whole series of quite exceptional details. The doorknocker on the main street door, the bell plaque, the number 48, are all elements which help to emphasise the highly urbane character of the ground floor, where Gaudí's furniture designs for the offices are work of the finest quality. If we step inside the hallway, we can see that it is divided up into compartments. Alter passing the first of these, the visitor is welcomed to the second by benches set against elliptical mirrors. A little further on, the ornamental complexity of the columns, the forerunners of the columns supporting the enclosed balcony in the Batlló house, come as a suprise, while the other, more baroque columns around the lift-cage recall a baldaquin which has been perforated to allow access to the different floors of the building. If we walk up to the first floor we can appreciate in detail the finish of the doors of the different apartments, with their peepholes and other pieces of metalwork, which deserve to be considered as pieces of jewellery.

We referred above to the somewhat unexceptional quality of the main facade, quite unlike the rear facade, which overlooks the courtyard in the interior of the block. In view of the difficulty of access, it will probably be necessary to rely on photographs to get to know this, in common with a number of Gaudí's other buildings. This is one of the few houses in the Barcelona Eixample where, thanks to Gaudí's commitment to his work, we have a facade with enclosed balconies coming off the living rooms, treated in similar fashion to the rear facade of the Palau Güell, together with balconies whose balustrades have been designed with great care and attention. It is worth dwelling on this point, since the approach generally adopted in the design of the rear facades of residential buildings in the Exiample is to use a continuous gallery, with more or less elaborate carpentry detailing, the aim being to ensure transparency above all and to take maximum advantage of the sun's light and warmth.

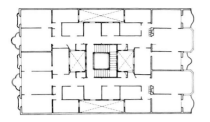

Typical floor and partial views
of the main facade

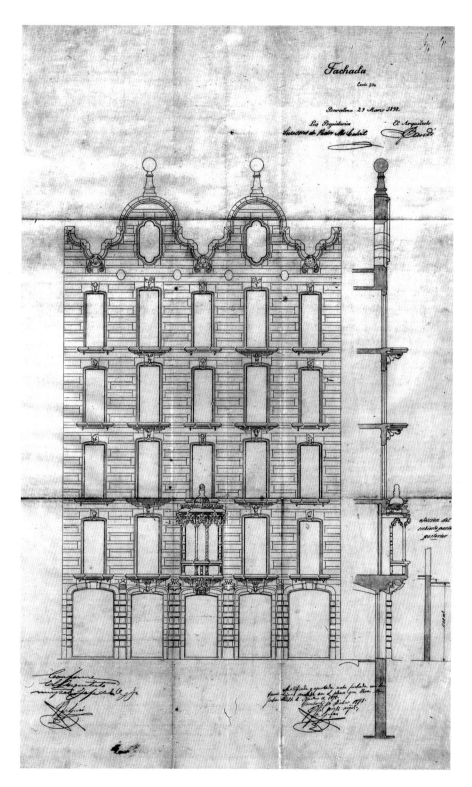

Detail of the parapet on the main facade, drawn by Carles Fochs, and details of the enclosed balcony and the number of the house

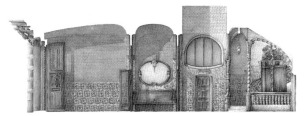

Transverse section through the hall, drawn by M.ª Isabel Herrero Campos, view of the rear facade and details of the doorhandle, the peephole and the lift

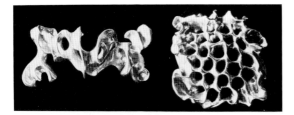

Following pages: details of the lift gates, the walls of the communal courtyard, the bell panel and doorknocker on the main door. Armchair, chair and sofa for the Calvet house

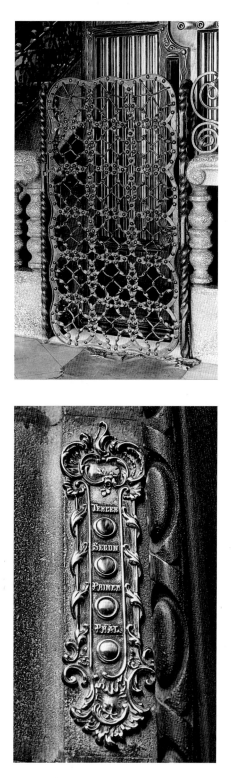

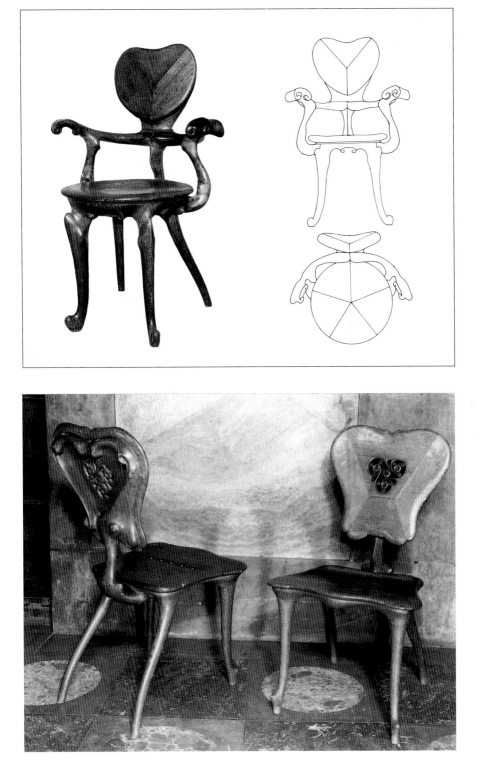

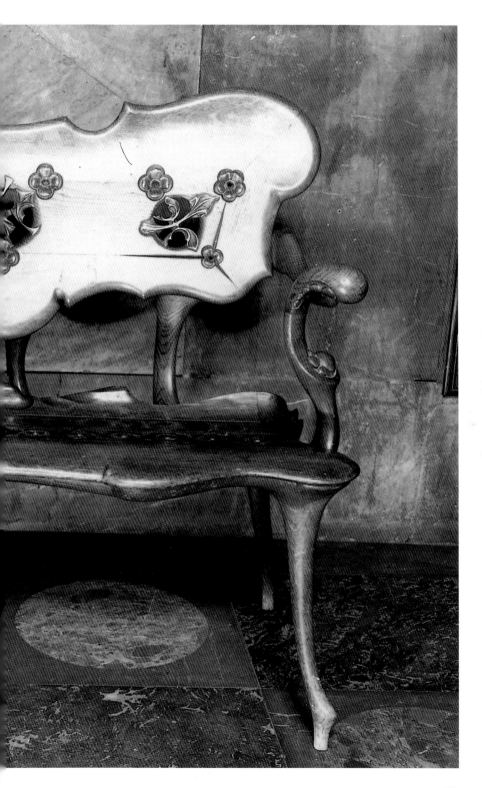

Torre Bellesguard house
1900-1905

C/ de Bellesguard, 16-20

VISITING: Private residence.

TRANSPORT: Buses 14, 22, 58, 64; FF.CC. Generalitat (Avinguda del Tibidabo).

POSITION ON THE PLAN: **6**

THE HOUSE STANDS IN AN AREA VERY close to the Collserola mountain, in the area where King Martí l'Humà, the last of the Catalan dynasty, had constructed his residence. In this project, Gaudí addressed himself to that great moment, the start of the new century. In this scheme, in which respect for the past is so prevalent, we can see how the house is raised up as an imposing volume, opaque and enclosed in itself, with Gaudí seeking to acknowledge the defensive character of the construction.

This idea of the isolated place, which must be defended, is preserved in the geminate and triform openings, which are tall and narrow, except in the area above the main entrance, where a sequence of balconies breaks this sheer, hard plane.

It is only on seeing the interior of the house, not easy to arrange in the case of a private residence such as this, that this hardness we have referred to is transformed into sweetness, in a setting that is peaceful, pleasant, legible and white. The upper part of the stairwell, just where it arrives at the attic level, is lit by a window which, with a geometrical composition and evident Arabic influences, bathes this upper area in different colours, at the same time leaving part of the space in shadow.

The attic under the roof, executed using brickwork arches with lightened facings, is a fine example of Gaudí's skill in the use of this material, and reveals the evolution of that skill in terms of form and construction. Once again, we must remark on the importance Gaudí attaches to the corners of his buildings, crowning them with turrets and spires, as he has done here, with the manifest purpose of

General view and view of the house from the garden

Plans and elevation, drawn by
Antonio Toscano González

perfectly supporting his four-armed cross,
which seems to be held aloft by some valiant
warrior.

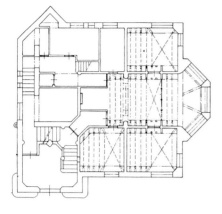

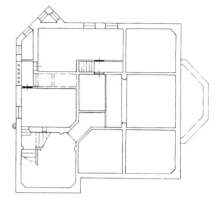

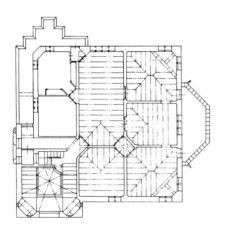

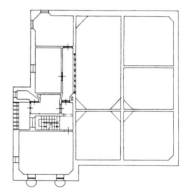

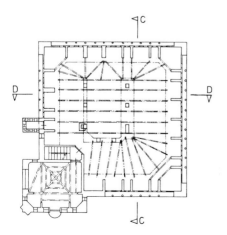

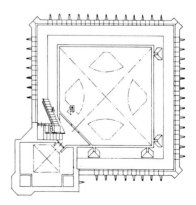

Following pages: views and
details of the facade, the view
from the turret, and
transverse section

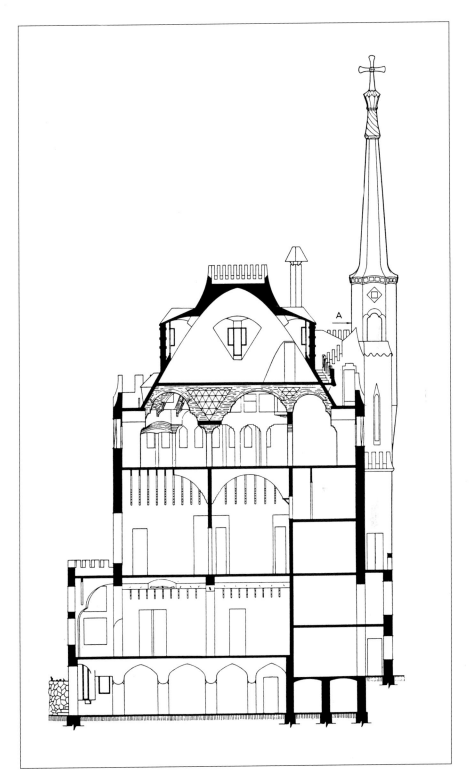

A

View of the basement and
details of the main door and
the interior of the staircase

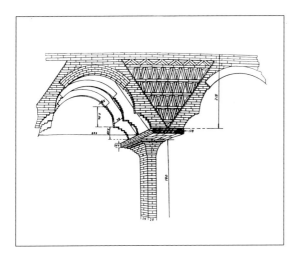

Details of the window over
the main door, the roof over
the stairwell, and the structure
of the attic

83

Various views of the brick
structure of the attic

Park Güell
1900-1914

C/ Olot, unnumbered

Collaborating architects:
Josep M.ª Jujol and Joan
Rubió i Bellver

VISITING: City park open to the public
during the hours of daylight.

TRANSPORT: Buses 24, 25.

POSITION ON THE PLAN: **7**

THIS IS THE LARGEST PIECE OF WORK, IN
terms of physical extension, Gaudí undertook
in Barcelona, on a 20 hectare site, which he
was to lay out and develop, equipping it with
services and, ultimately, convert into a garden
city along the lines of the ones which had
appeared in England during the second half of
the 19th century. It is for this reason that the
English 'Park' was used in preference to the
Catalan 'Parc'.

Park Güell is the most important piece of
work which Gaudí carried out in the entire
course of his career as an architect, in that it
is the most complete. In its execution, he was
able to count on the collaboration of the
architect Josep Mª Jujol on all those elements
which involved colour. In this project, we must
consider the architectonic aspects of the two
pavilions which frame the main entrance on
carrer Olot: these undoubtedly deserve to be
regarded as unique in their own right, and yet
at the same time they allow us to establish
some degree of comparison with the pavilions
for the Güell estate on the avinguda de
Pedralbes, in view of the similarity of
conception which exists between them. The
major pieces of design work in Park Güell
assume an unusual potency, as in the case of
the hypostile hall which supports the large
plaza with the sinuous bench around its
perimeter. Finally, we ought not to overlook
those aspects of the project which imitate the
topography of their setting, in the form of the
viaducts, the elevated walkways and certain
individual elements such as the palm trees,
which act as references to their environment.

Another point of interest is Gaudí's
approach to the urban design of the Park, in
considering this residential area as an
enclosed, defended space. To a certain
extent, the possibility of the citizens of
Barcelona making use of and enjoying this
park was at the time fairly limited, particularly
in view of its location, which was then
somewhat remote and inaccessible. A few
years later the place was acquired by the city
authorities and, more recently, in 1984,
UNESCO declared it a part of the world's
heritage.

Having noted these points, we can go on
to give a general commentary on Park Güell.
The two pavilions by the main entrance, the

one on the left designed as the gatekeeper's residence, the one on the right as a waiting room and meeting point for visitors, ought to be considered as two quite unique pieces of work. In connecting these two buildings by means of the stone wall, Gaudí wanted them to be understood in terms of two cylindrical towers, jealously protecting the enclosure and its residential development. This intimation of a Mediaeval spirit (inward-looking and secretive) is brought perfectly up to date with the introduction of colour, precisely at the point where he presents us with this image of the unassailable tower. The warped contours of the surfaces, crowned with the mushroom of which Gaudí was so fond, the "Amanita Muscaria", and covered with the *trencadis* of ceramic fragments, creating a formal composition which takes on geometric qualities as it moulds these roofs, are in themselves sufficient to class Gaudí as an architect of genius.

The presence alongside each other of these two pavilions and the space which leads on to the flight of steps, where we find a

General plan of the park:
1. Hillock with the Calvary, originally intended as site for the Chapel
2. Former Güell residence, now converted for use as a municipal school
3. Hall of pseudo-Doric columns, intended as the market for the planned residential development
4. Large open plaza, partly on solid ground, partly built over the hypostile hall
5. Gaudí's chalet-house
6. Chalet-house belonging to Dr. Trías
A. Portico adjoining the Güell residence, with raised walkway
B. Portico with three series of columns and raised walkway
C. Portico with three series of columns in triangular distribution and raised walkway with rustic seating and tall planters
D. Portico with double series of columns and raised walkway

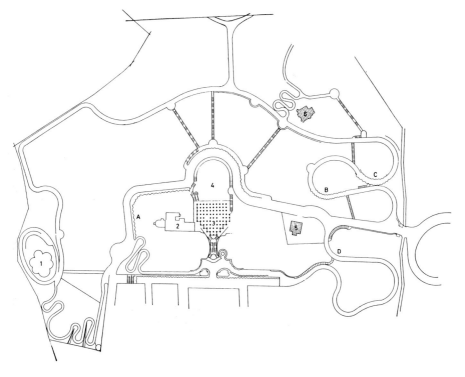

Medallions and views of the pavilion by the main gate

fountain and the figure of a salamander, all clad in *trencadís*, charmingly accompanies us up to the great hypostile hall, which Gaudí conceived as the ideal location for the fresh food market which would serve the residents of the development exclusively. Note, too, the four medallions with their adjoining motifs, which take the place of four of the columns.

Continuing on our ascending itinerary, we arrive at the great platform which situates us over the Barcelona plain. We should pay particular attention here to the serpentine outline of the perimeter, which takes the form of a bench which, thanks to the vibrant quality of the intense light it receives, manages to create a sensation of movement. If we bear in mind that Gaudí consistently uses animal and plantlife as a point of reference in his architecture, we begin to understand this great serpent with its distinctive silhouette and texture like snakeskin which basks in a privileged position under the heat of the sun and the intense light of the Mediterranean.

The ceramic cladding, based on broken pieces of tile, debris, and at certain points, fragments of plates, china dolls and glass wine jars, converts this bench, intended for relaxation, conversation and rest, into an immense collage without precedent.

Finally, we must mention those elements which constitute the infrastructure necessary to be able to reach all the different parts of the park: viaducts, retaining walls, elevated walkways and various one-off elements.

The viaducts are a good example of the dialogue established with the natural topography of the place, at times acquiring a symbolic weight, at others no more than simple cylindrical columns which harmonise perfectly with the structural logic. They are all built of local stone, roughly finished, but perfectly positioned. In those places where the ivy acts as interlocutor, the stones are small; where the wall has to be strong, it is inclined, forming a chiaroscuro with classical roots, and the stony mass is rougher. Where there are curves with an appreciable change in level we find columns which, like modelled spirals, indicate a change and a movement. Where the way is smoother, planters engage in a dialogue with the palms, with these even registering a change between trunk and treetop. Where the way takes on a more agile movement, becoming an elevated walk or bridge, the planters which accompany and protect its path are exceptionally tall, while the paving, like a continuous carpet, provides a constant point of reference.

Detail of the flight of steps leading to the hypostile hall

Plans and elevation of the
pavilions, and details of the
wrought iron railings and the
roof. Plan and elevation of the
roof of the gatekeeper's
lodge, drawn by L. Montero

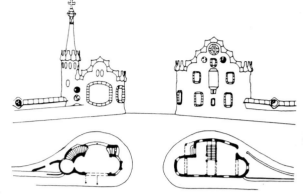

Pages 94-95: detail of the
turret of the pavilion and the
spiral spire with its rectangular
pattern, and elevation, drawn
by Concepción Rodríguez
Arribas

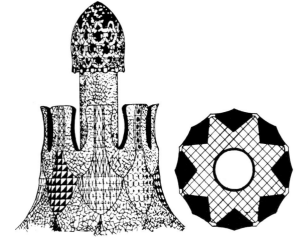

Pages 96/97: details of the roofs of the two pavilions and aerial view of the bench and the spire of the gatehouse

Pages 98/99: partial views of the colonnade of the hypostile hall and the bench

Previous pages: view of the
interior space of the hypostile
hall

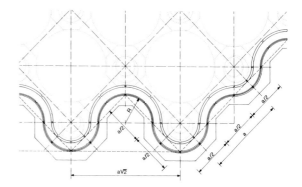

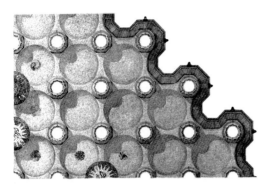

Modular plans of the bench, drawn by I. Paricio, and of the roof of the hypostile hall, drawn by Núria Llaverias Baques, views of the columns and outline from below, and partial view of the bench

Following pages: detail of the "trencadís" of the bench

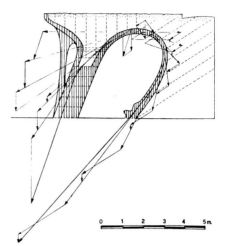

Views of the porticoes, details of the
entrance door to a portico, a sculpture and
the planters. Section with diagram of loads
and thrusts, drawn by Joan Bergós, and plan
and sections of the portico, drawn by Ruiz
Vallés, Morilla, Pellicer, Recasens Sarabia
and Villanueva

Wall and gate for the Miralles estate
1901-1902

Passeig Manuel Girona, 55-61

TRANSPORT: Buses 6, 16, 34, 66, 70, 74; Metro L3 (Maria Cristina)

POSITION ON THE PLAN: **8**

IN THIS BOUNDARY WALL WE CAN detect a certain resemblance, if we study the outline, to that of Park Güell, albeit in somewhat simplified form. Gaudí introduces a wide central opening for horsedrawn vehicles, and a second, smaller opening for pedestrians.

The treatment of the gate as an opening in the wall reinforces the idea of the wall's continuity. The strain of the upper part of the roof covering the ensemble, of fine concrete tiles manufactured by the owner of the estate, is taken by steel cables which converge on the four-armed cross characteristic of Gaudí.

Views of the gate and details of the railings of the side door, the wall, and the roof seen from below

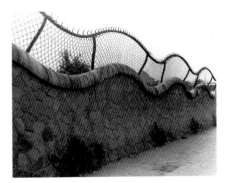

Batlló house
1904-1906

Passeig de Gràcia, 43.

Collaborating architect:
Josep Mª Jujol

VISITING: Weekdays from 8.00 to
10.00, by prior arrangement with the
Càtedra Gaudí (from 8.00 to 14.00.
Tel. 204 52 50).

Transport: Buses 7, 22, 24, 58; Metro
L3 (Passeig de Gràcia).

POSITION ON THE PLAN: 9

General view of the main
facade, adjoining the Ametller
house by the architect Josep
Puig i Cadafalch

THIS HOUSE, AND THE CALVET HOUSE
in carrer Casp, are the only examples in
Gaudí's work of apartment buildings on gap
sites with a single facade, some 15 metres
wide, in the Barcelona Eixample.

Before going on to analyse this scheme,
we should take note of two facts of
importance. The first concerns the Ametller
house, to the left, with its grand stepped
parapet reminiscent of Fleminsh architecture;
this was completed in 1900, just six years
previously, by the architect Josep Puig i
Cadafalch. The second, a little more complex,
is that the Batlló house is a conversion of a
previously existing building. In other words, in
carrying out his project for this house, Gaudí
had to transform and extend the building
already occupying the site. Precisely on
account of this work of transformation and
change, Gaudí found himself involved in one
of the most interesting projects in his career
as an architect. Specifically, this work
consisted of the addition of two floors to the
existing house, the application of a new
exterior skin to front and rear, and, finally, the
adaptation of the main floor as residence for
the family of José Batlló Casanovas.

The increase in the height of this
apartment building was an undertaking which
Gaudí aproached in such a way as to give it a
greater slenderness. The second of the two
floors he added figures only on the front
facade, being in effect a crown with an
irregular outline in the form of a shell, with two
separate faces linked by a suture made up of
armatures of glazed ceramic, with a distinctly
mediaeval appearance. The cylindrical turret
topped by the four-armed cross provides the
counterpoint which balances and regulates the
meeting of the silhouettes of the two houses.

The change in the building's skin can be
properly understood only by considering the
majority of facades then to be seen in this part
of the Eixample. Gaudí, who on this occasion
enlisted the help of Josep M.ª Jujol, the young
architect who was to become profoundly
involved in a number of other projects,
performed an operation whereby he replaced
the existing skin on this facade and at the
same time projected an enclosed balcony from
the main floor; this features bone-like elements
which, with something skeletal about them, are

Plan of the main floor, typical
floor plan and front and rear
elevation, drawn by Lluís
Bonet Garí

in evident contrast to the neighbouring house. The new skin, with its undulating movement, is a beautiful and exemplary exercise in the illumination of a facade in the manner of the book illustrators of the Middle Ages.

The change effected in the rear facade, which is visible from the passageway opening out near the chamfered corner on carrer Aragó, is simpler, since here Gaudí has limited himself to the design of balconies whose modelled fretwork balustrades follow their sinuous movement. The adaptation of the main floor is also an examplary piece of work, in the design of all the various elements which combine to form a dwelling: the stairway, entirely of wood; the internal doors, some opaque, some with glazed sections, which act as convex partitions with moveable screens, their profiles continually avoiding the rectilinear; the ceilings, such as the one in the main drawing room, which has a centrifugal form which seeks to focus attention on the element which illuminates the room; the wooden floors, the fireplaces, as well as a new suite of furniture for the dining room... All in all, this is a repertoire of perfectly thought-out solutions for a unique setting.

Finally, we must not overlook the space corresponding to the lightwells and ventilation shafts, which ascend from the vestibule on the ground floor to the great skylight which covers these voids and protects the blue and white tiles on their walls from the rain: ceramic tiles whose blue gradually changes in quality, distributing light through these two wells so that the lower part of the space receives the maximum possible intensity of natural light.

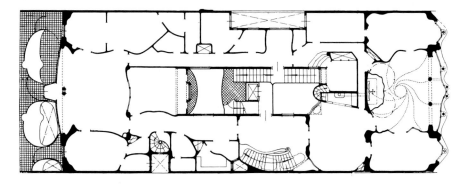

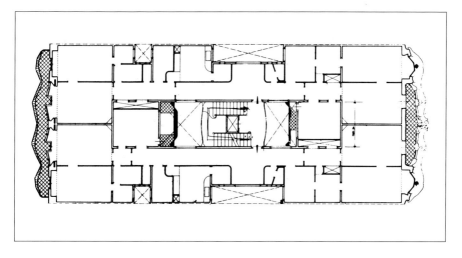

Details and partial views of
the facade and the enclosed
balcony on the main floor

117

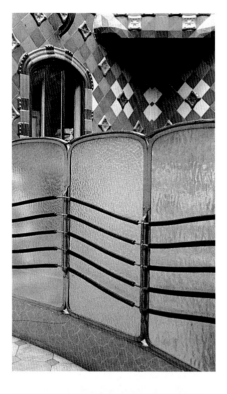

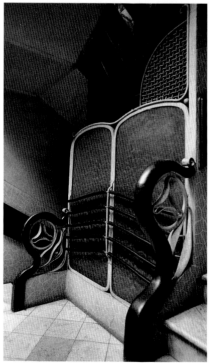

Previous pages: views of the chimneys and the rear facade

Details of the door, partitions and skylight over the stairwell

View of the original interior of
the dining room on the main
floor

Following pages: various
views of the main floor in its
original state

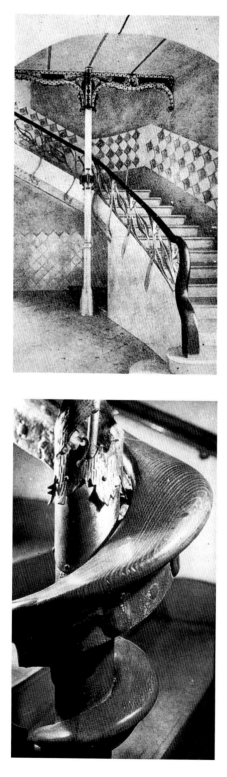

Various views of the two staircases and the interior of the main floor with the double armchair

Views of furniture and fittings
from the Batlló house

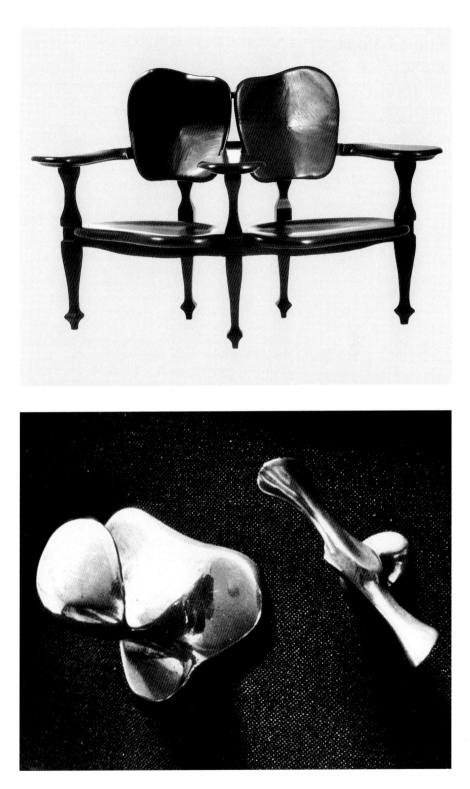

Milà i Camps house, "La Pedrera"

1906-1910

Passeig de Gràcia, 92 -
c/ Provença, 261-265

Collaborating architects:
Domènec Sugranyes,
Josep Canaleta and Josep
Mª Jujol

VISITING: Weekdays from 10.00 to
13.00 and 17.00 to 19.00. Saturdays
from 10.00 to 13.00.

TRANSPORT: Buses 22, 24; Metro L3
and L5 (Diagonal).

POSITION ON THE PLAN: **10**

IN TERMS OF CHRONOLOGICAL sequence, this is the third and last of the residential buildings Gaudí construted in the Barcelona Eixample, and the only one to occupy a site on a "xamfrà" or chamfered corner. Accordingly, the house can be considered as having three facades: one on each street, and the third on the corner, forming a 45° angle with each of the others.

The point of departure in Gaudí's approach to this grand facade lies in his treating it as single and continuous. If we fix our attention on some of the other houses on the passeig de Gràcia, we can see that in most cases there is a determination to register the change of plane, in terms of its disposition with respect to the passeig de Gràcia, the lateral street or the 'xamfrà'. The only concession Gaudí has made is to give the building two entrances, one on carrer Provença, the other on the chamfered corner. With the provision of these two entrances, the building is then to be understood in the following manner; each entrance consists of a smaller doorway for pedestrians and a larger door for carriages. This fact, which may at first seem unimportant, has consequences of considerable significance.

If we pursue the question of the two vehicular and pedestrian entrances in greater detail, we can see that the two courtyards which are so perfectly connected to them have all the imoportance of a second facade, with the difference that, while the dominant characteristic of the exterior facade is its horizontal undulation, in the interior courtyards the dominant structure is vertical and virtually regular, the height of each floor being constant, with the exception of the taller main floor, another unusual feature in the houses of the Eixample. If we continue with the two large polychrome vestibules, we see that the only means of reaching the main floor is by way of a grand flight of stairs, comparable to the one in the Batlló house, with no general staircase to communicate the different apartments in a more regular, orderly fashion. This function is carried out by two spacious lifts, situated by the two main entrances, while the general staircase is relegated to a role of much lesser importance, as the service stairs.

Another point worth observing is the facade

and the slight backward angle of the plane which crowns it, white on this attic level, as the perfect support for the spinning tops which greet us on arriving at this belvedere with its disconcerting forms which bear such a startling resemblance to the figures of warriors.

Again as in the Batlló house, Gaudí takes particular pleasure in the design of protective elements such as grilles, doors and balustrades. On this occasion, with the inestimable collaboration of Jujol, he resolves all of these features to perfection. The balustrades on the balconies are at their finest here, not only on account of their lightness contrasted with the mass of stone, but for their dramatic potential, starting from a band which twists around itself in truly provocative manner.

Partial view of the main facade

Typical floor plan, drawn by
César Martinelli, and various
views of the house before
and after completion

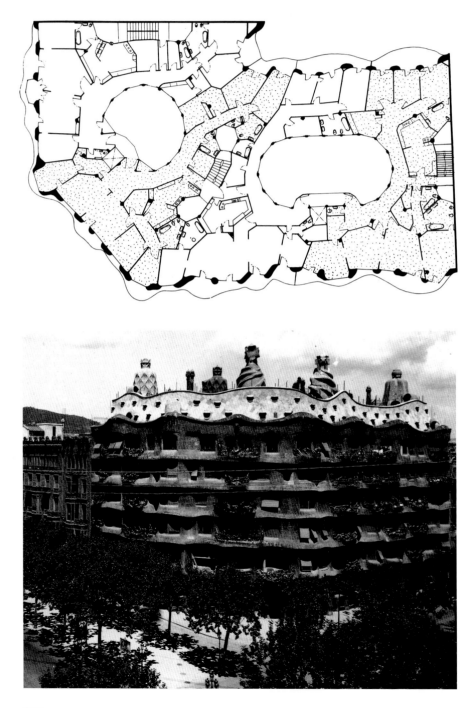

Partial views of the main facade and details of a ceiling in one of the apartments and the paving of pressed mosaic

Following pages: partial views of the main facade with the balustrades of the balconies by the architect Josep M. Jujol and detail of some of the chimneys and the volumes which mark the arrival of the staircase at roof level

Previous pages: view of the vestibule area
of the circular courtyard in 1914

Partial views and details of the vestibule and
inner courtyard

Previous pages: views of the
courtyard of the Provença
entrance and the circular
courtyard

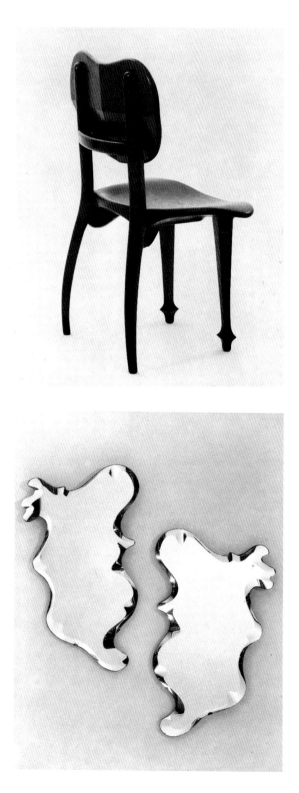

Examples of the furnishings:
office chair, a pair of mirrors,
a mirror with a gilt wooden
frame and a wood and glass
screen

Transverse section through
the circular courtyard, drawn
by the Gaudí Groep of Delft,
section of the parabolic arch
of the roof space, plan of the
roof structure, and views of
the roof space before it was
modified in the 1950s, and of
the interior during construction and on completion

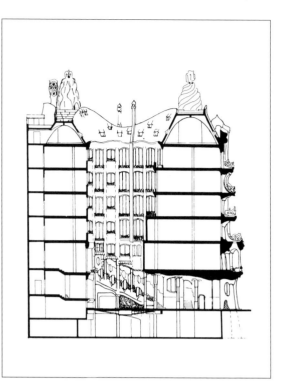

Sagrada Familia schoolrooms
1909-1910

C/ Marina, 253 - plaça Gaudí

VISITING: Daily from 9.00 to 19.00.

TRANSPORT: Buses 19, 34, 43, 50, 51, 54; Metro L5 (Sagrada Familia).

POSITION ON THE PLAN: **11**

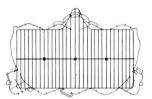

THIS LITTLE BUILDING, PROVISIONAL and temporary in character, located on the same block as the temple, was designed in response to strict criteria of cost and speed of construction. With a surface area of two hundred square metres, 10 × 20 m, and the possibility of being subdivided into a number of different classrooms, Gaudí here apllies the sinuous, undulating line once again, but this time as the containing form; in other words, it is used here for wall and roof.

The structure, of great simplicity, is resolved on the basis of pillars which support a central longitudinal profile which holds up the framework of the roof; this rests on the rising and falling line of the sloping wall, which is thus responsible for its undulating plane.

The whole structure is built of solid handmade brick. The door and window openings require lateral rebating, since the thickness of the wall is minimal.

Its fragility, its freedom of division of the interior space to suit the needs of the moment, the exemplary skill with which the form and volumetry of a building so modest in its overall dimensions have been handled, entitle this minor piece of work to special consideration.

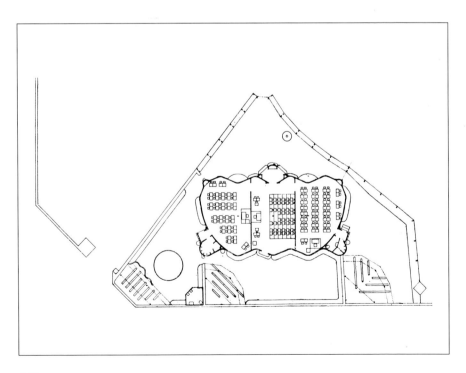

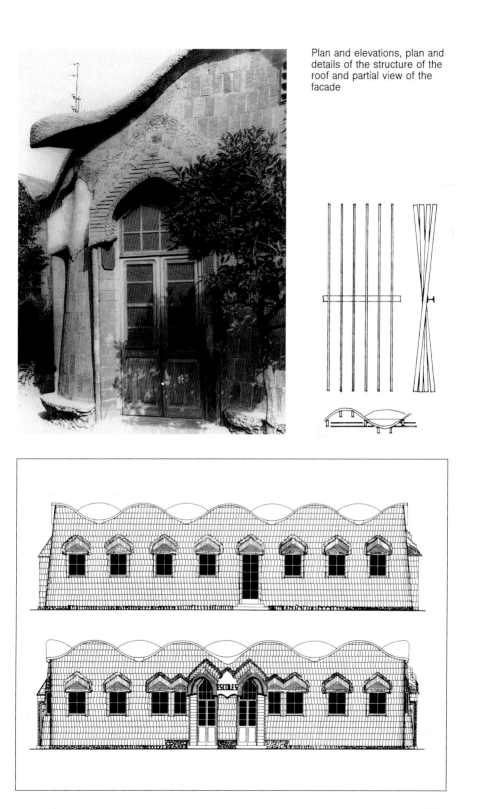

Plan and elevations, plan and details of the structure of the roof and partial view of the facade

Expiatory Temple of the Sagrada Familia
1883-1926

C/ Marina, 253 - plaça Gaudí

VISITING: Daily from 9.00 to 19.00.

TRANSPORT: Buses 19, 34, 43, 50, 51, 54; Metro L5 (Sagrada Familia).

POSITION ON THE PLAN: **12**

ON THE 3RD OF OCTOBER, 1883, AT THE age of 31, Gaudí accepted the commission to carry on the work of building the new cathedral for Barcelona, begun by the architect Francisco de Paula Villar y Lozano, an honour for which he was recommended by the architect Joan Martorell. For obvious reasons, Gaudí was to combine his dedication to this project with the other pieces of work which he undertook during his forty-three years of professional activity.

Nonetheless, we must note that the last ten years of his life were affected by the frailty of his health, which from 1910 on obliged him to rest for long periods.

Before going on to describe the work Gaudí carried out on the temple, I believe a brief description of the project as a whole is called for. The Expiatory Temple of the Sagrada Familia is based on a plan in the form of a Latin cross, composed of five naves, an apse and a transept. The main nave and the transept have lengths of 95 and 60 metres respectively. The width of the central nave is 15 metres, while the side naves are half this width, and the transept measures 30 m across.

A reading or study of the plan of the temple allows us to discern that it should have three facades, facing east, south and west: the Nativity, Glory and Passion facades.

On the other, north-facing side is the apse, which comprises seven chapels and an ambulatory. Each of these facades is composed of ample porticoes, which are crowned in turn by four towers set in pairs to leave a wedgeshaped central space to be occupied by a sculptural element; the average height of these bell towers is 100 metres.

To mark the centre of the transept, an immense dome 170 metres high aspires to the role of symbol, identifying the temple. The respective heights of the central and lateral naves were to be, according to the project, 45 and 30 metres. If we study the transverse section, reproduced in the introduction to this book, we can see that in the lateral naves, at a height some halfway up the nave, Gaudí has included galleries for groups of singers.

Finally, we ought to note the idea of the peripheral cloister which Gaudí sought to introduce into the scheme for the temple, intending this space to act as a kind of buffer between the city and the interior of the church.

Just before we go on to describe the project as it stands, I would like to offer an assessment which I feel to be of some importance. Gaudí took on the responsibility of continuing a building which, in view of its scale, he was unlikely to see completed. Yet, this consideration aside, which has more to do with means and dedication, Gaudí undertook a thorough review of the project, rethinking its principles to such an extent that, while stopping short of demolishing any of what had already been built, nevertheless completely transformed Villar's utterly neo-Gothic conception of the church. Gaudí moves on beyond Viollet-le-Duc's theories here, in the sense that he not only accepts the construction as a reconstruction and attempts to make it perfect, but he goes one step further and responds to the imperative need to evolve, to develop out of a style which is undoubtedly lacking in secrets, and in which his involvement would be practically anonymous, as is the case with so many other cathedrals and churches.

In studying the structural behaviour of Gothic architecture, Gaudí came to believe

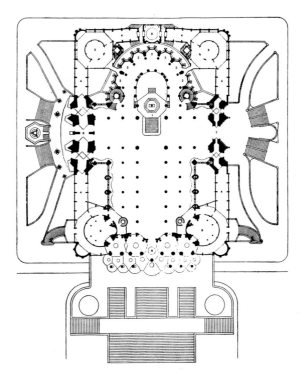

General plan

that this could be simplified, employing new
approaches which would result in a more
daring, innovative design. In dispensing with
lateral buttresses, he utilises the tiered
galleries as an element with a similar function,
but in the interior. This solution was to allow
him to give a much sheerer treatment to the
side facades, and thus ensure that the bell
towers on each facade, being slightly set back
into the interior of the temple, give it a more
vertical configuration.

Gaudí had to wait until 1900 to see part of
the interior facade of the Nativity raised into
place. Here we find nothing but geometry and
architecture. The vision, in its entirety as well
as in detail, is a progress through a multitude
of stone volumes whose forms and proportions
are quite disparate. It is essential to know how
to understand this vision composed of
fragments. It is easy to be distracted by its
monumental character, yet in contrast to the
opposite face of the temple, it is here, in the
attentive contemplation of this skeleton, that
we can see a distinctive, unique manifestation
of the evolution of Gaudí's work. The design of
this facade was completed in 1917. Up until

1926, Gaudí was working on sketches for the chapel of the Assumption of the Virgin, situated in the peripheral cloister, for the sacristies on either side of the apse, new stained glass windows, and the structure of the vaults, as well as studies for the columns, in which Gaudí carried out an astonishing process of analysis and revision, changing their silhouette by means of a breakdown of their geometry piece by piece, each piece having the same diameter, from which he constructed the columns in their great height.

In 1915, Joan Rubió made a sketch of the temple complex as a whole in which the general dimensions can be appreciated.

When Gaudí died in 1926, the pinnacles of the four towers on the Nativity facade had still to be completed, and those who had worked most closely with him immediately saw to it that these were finished. After the hiatus of the Spanish Civil War, from 1936 to 1939, construction work on the temple was resumed by a multi-disciplinary team of technicians and craftsmen faithful to Gaudí's conception, although this has necessarily progressed slowly on account of the high cost of the work.

Following pages: part of the section of the project by F. P. Villar y Lozano. View of the crypt modified by Gaudí and scale study in comparison with the basilica of Saint Peter's in Rome

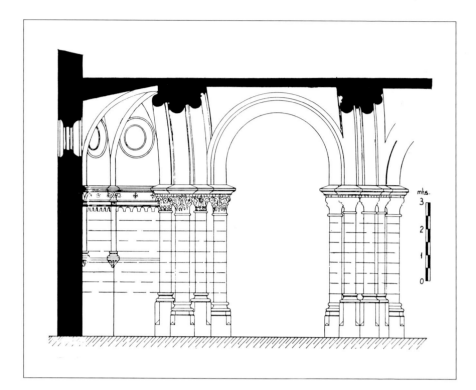

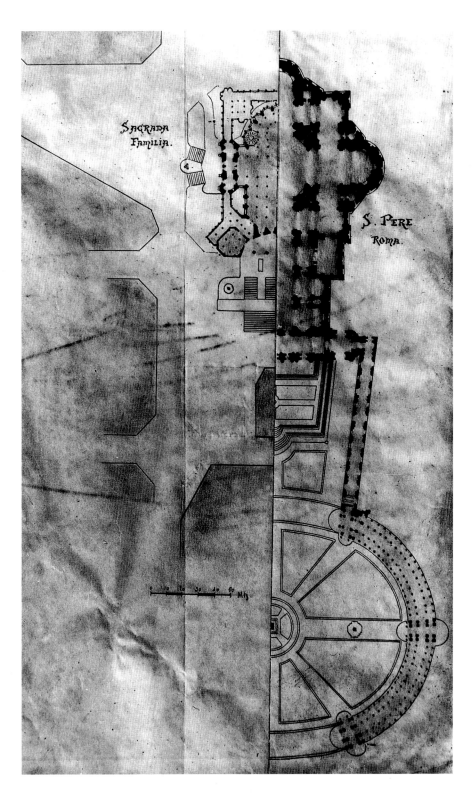

SAGRADA
FAMILIA.

S. PERE
ROMA.

0 10 20 30 40 50 Mh

153

View of the model of the Nativity facade, sketch of the project, drawn by Joan Rubió i Bellver in 1915, and general view of the temple

Following pages: partial views of the Nativity facade and the bell towers

157

Previous pages: partial views of the Nativity facade and the bell towers

Various views of the bell towers and partial view of the interior of the Nativity facade

Partial views of the pinnacles of the bell towers, view of the interior staircase, and elevations showing the free geometrical rhythm of the pinnacles

Following pages: various pieces of furniture from the temple, details of the interior of the Nativity facade and sketch of the Passion facade drawn by Gaudí

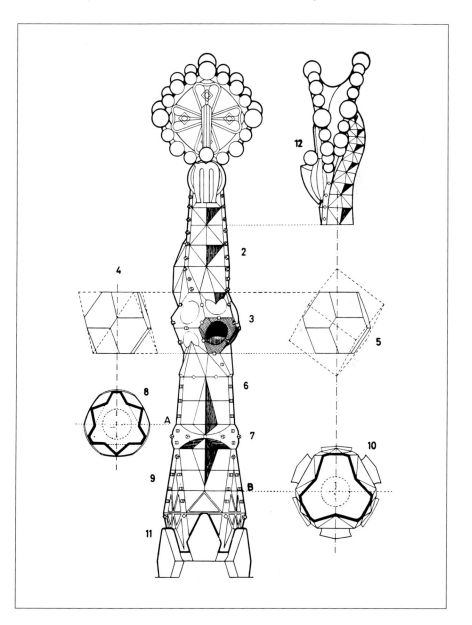

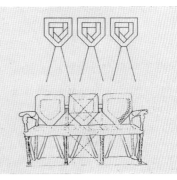

Crypt for the Colonia Güell
1898-1908-1915

Santa Coloma de Cervelló
(Baix Llobregat,
Barcelona)

Collaborating architects:
Josep Canaleta and
Francesc Berenguer

LOCATION: On the main road to Sant
Boi de Llobregat at Sant Vicenç dels
Horts.

VISITING: The complex is always
open.

TRANSPORT: Bus from Barcelona
(Plaça Espanya), L 70 (Ciutat
Cooperativa de Sant Boi); FF.CC.
Generalitat (direction Santa Coloma -
get off at Molí Nou station).

View of the crypt under
construction and plan of the
roof structure, drawn by Lluís
Bonet

GAUDÍ WAS COMMISSIONED BY EUSEBI
Güell in 1898 to build a church for the textile
workers' colony on his estate. In the ten years
that followed, Gaudí produced an endless
number of drawings and models in his studies
of how to resolve the church's structure.

Gaudí wanted to arrive at a synthesis of
all the forces which enter into play in a
building. He very carefully analysed the
structural behaviour of Gothic churches, but
his aim was to move on from Gothic, reducing
the columns and buttresses, to find a single
structural element capable of absorbing all the
forces applied to it. He therefore reduced all of
the component parts to create a unique form
which, although inclined, and geometrically
unusual, provided him with a new solution to
the treatment of the building.

We know of the existence of only a
couple of sketches showing Gaudí's vision of
the church as a whole, of which only the crypt
was actually built. In this building, the desire
for expression attains its greatest splendour. If
we consider the interior space, we see that it
can be analysed in terms of two areas: a first,
central area, taking in the altar, and a second
area, in the form of an ambulatory, which
follows the line of the perimeter in a U-shaped
movement.

In looking at the first area, it is important
to note the roof structure, supported on four
inclined columns and a wall in the form of a
main apse and its annexes which define this
first area.

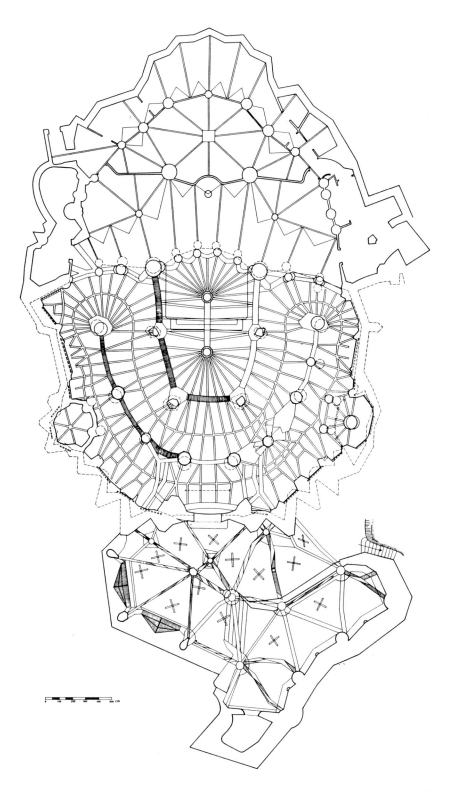

In the second area, which surrounds the first, we can see how a double circulation system is organised around the central transept, this being reflected in the roof structure by a turn of 180°. This form does not, however, correspond to the actual use of the crypt, since the whole of the interior functions as a single space. These two spaces we have described occupy approximatelly half of the plan.

The difference between the interior and exterior of this building is of considerable significance. While the interior is required to focus the attention on a single point, the altar, the reading of the exterior is somewhat difficult, since the surrounding woods tend to camouflage and conceal what should be the base, the socle of the building. The treatment of the successive porticoes of the porch is admirable, with these seeking to continue the somewhat random distribution of the trees around them.

The roof of the porch has been treated with a smoothness and colouration which suggest a coppice of trees. The eleven slanting columns which make up this porch all have different textures, and have all been treated differently, as if with the intention of enriching the surrounding pinewood with the addition of new species, and create the perfect prologue to the interior space. The various different triangular areas to be seen on the roof of this portico, the treatment of which is modulated through the use of a combination of glazed ceramic and matt-finished elements, all of them set flush with the stonework, set up a dialogue with the buttresses and the outer skin of the crypt.

The texture of the stone on the exterior, which almost seems to be trying to hide behind the thick ivy, is crowned by cavities which recall various forms of the human body. These openings contain the stained glass windows which, with their variety of geometrical forms, almost always including a cross in movement, give the interior its great diversity of colour as the sun moves across the sky. The air of mystery which the crypt might have as an empty building is transformed by the presence of the furniture, principally the small bench or pew, which articulates the interior space.

In the adjoining gardens the stone columns which were to have supported the roof of the upper floor lie full-length, like tombstones.

In this crypt for the Colonia Güell, Gaudí sums up all of his past efforts in an attempt at establishing his own personal dialogue with his work, while avoiding any association which might be inappropriate to the project in hand. He rejects the temptation to rely on established canons, in pursuit of a thoroughly

General plan of the Colonia Güell and partial view of the entrance

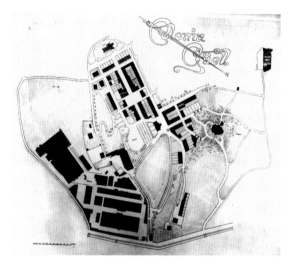

Sketches of the exterior and interior by Gaudí

expressive architecture, and he unquestionably succeeds in the formal results he obtains; in spite of the fact that this is his most daring piece of work, it is here that he achieves complete and absolute recognition.

Following pages: stereometric
model showing loads and
stresses and front and side
views of the entrance portico

Previous pages: partial views
of the roof and columns of the
entrance portico

Views of the portico and the
side facade with the stained
glass windows

Elevation of a window, interior view of the crypt during construction, the entrance portico with the woods beyond and view of the interior

Following pages: views of the columns lying between the trees in the wood, the interior, and detail of a window and a bench

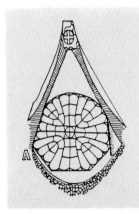

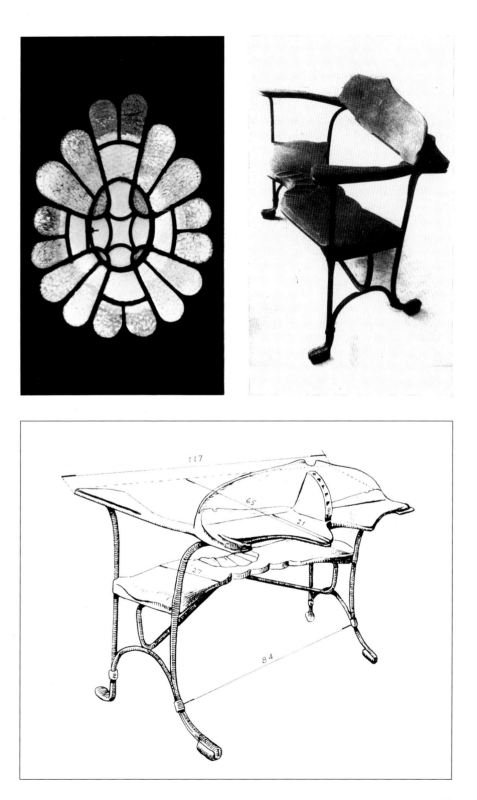

Work built outside Barcelona

El Capricho villa
1883-1885

Comillas, Santander

VISITING: Restaurant open seven days a week

THIS SUMMER VILLA FOR DON MÁXIMO Díaz de Quijano, adjacent to the palace of the Marqués de Comillas, and contemporary with the Vicens house, exhibits the same stylistic influences, but with a somewhat different programme, distributed over a half-basement, a main floor and an attic under the roof. The entrance, situated at one corner of the house, is clearly identified by a tall cylindrical tower made of brick and clad in glazed ceramic tiles, the lower part of which metamorphoses into a porch with four columns, while the upper part is crowned by a belvedere which declares itself as the most evocative element of the whole composition. Gaudí continues here to explore and expand on the corner belvedere element, giving free rein to his creativity in the treatment of benches which also serve as a balustrade, here with a smoother and more uniform decorative formalism than in the Vicens house. The simultaneous use of courses of hand-made brick and strips of glazed ceramic tile in higher relief completes the outer skin of the house. Here, the windows are set flush with the plane of the facade, with a very pronounced vertical division, while on the inside the bays provide space for seating.

The on-site supervision and direction of the construction work was carried out by Cristóbal Cascante and Camil Oliveras, fellow students of Gaudí's at the Escuela de Arquitectura de Barcelona.

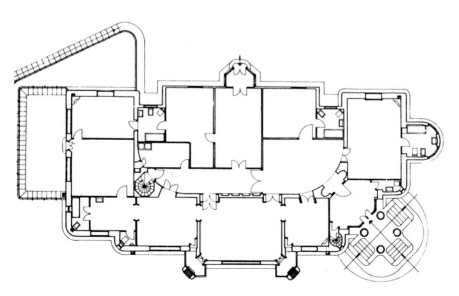

General view and various details of the belvedere, the window and the ceramic cladding

Episcopal Palace

1887-1893

Astorga (León)

AFTER THE DESTRUCTION BY FIRE OF the original episcopal residence, Gaudí received the commission to construct the new palace. The building consists of a basement, ground floor, main floor and attic.

All of the exterior walls which make up the building's various facades were constructed of grey granite, while in the interior Gaudí used loadbearing walls, pillars with capitals and cross-vaulting, as well as ogival arches.

With the exception of the main entrance, which has a portico with splaying arches, the rest of the building exhibits a high degree of compositional unity. The various turrets which lend even greater emphasis to the verticality give continuity to the external aspect of the building, employing the formal device of neo-mediaevalism in the treatment of the corners. The force thus conferred on the mass of stone gives the work as a whole an excessively overpowering effect.

Once again, we can only lament the fact that Gaudí did not himself finish the building, since, on the death of the archbishop who awarded him the brief, Gaudí declined to supervise the construction work. Thus the Episcopal Palace in Astorga is a work attributable only in part to Antoni Gaudí. This fact makes itself fully apparent to the observer, even although the people who actually finished off the project made every effort to follow the scheme drawn up by Gaudí.

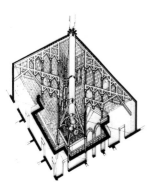

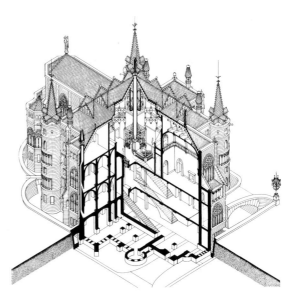

Axonometric sketch, sections and various views of the palace and its surroundings

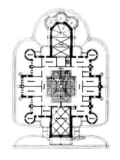

Plan and various details of the exterior and interior

Fernández Andrés house ("Los Botines")

1891-1894

Plaza del Obispo Marcelo, León

THIS FREE-STANDING BUILDING WHICH Gaudí constructed in the old centre of the historic city of León is a good illustration of the period of doubt and uncertainty in which he found himself immersed at the time. Here we can see him refining the neo-Gothic language which he had already used in earlier schemes.

By the time he came to design this building, Gaudí could claim a certain familiarity with the place in which it was to stand. Nevertheless, the project to a large extent ignores its surroundings, including a number of important buildings, and introduces a previously unknown architecture into León. The way in which the masonry is handled, the cylindrical enclosed balconies, with the clearly French influence in their spires and their excessive volume, invalidate this scheme in terms of the context in which it is situated. However, this degree of formal incoherence is overcome in the resolution of the scheme. The first instance of this is to be found on the ground floor, with its fan of cylindrical pillars which are perfectly in tune with their setting, creating an ambulatory between the outer skin of the building and the first corridor, a formal device which Gaudí was to utilise to masterly effect in the Park Güell.

The other floors intended for use as living quarters, with their brickwork structure, adhere perfectly to the layout of the ground floor. The facades, in which the organisation of the openings is conceived in such a way that the matched pairs of windows on the first floor enter into play with others of lesser importance, are crowned by the volume of the slate roof.

Elevation and general views of the main facade

194

Various views of the house and its surroundings and details of the main door and the railings

Restoration work on Palma Cathedral
1903-1914

Palma de Mallorca

Collaborating architects:
Joan Rubió i Bellver
and Josep M. Jujol

VISITING: Open for church services

Views of the pulpit and the presbytery from the central nave

Following pages: various details of the grand baldachine-chandelier and the painting on the choir stall

GAUDÍ'S CONTRIBUTION TO THIS building ought to be considered in two parts. The first was limited to the work of reorganising the internal functioning of the church, shifting the choir to the presbytery and bringing the altar forward. The second, and more important, intervention is effectively composed of four phases or sections: Jujol's decoration of the choir stall with paintings and carvings based on plant forms, the baldachine-chandelier, the pulpit and the stained glass windows.

With regard to Jujol's decorative painting, the only possible response is simple admiration of a piece of work which, although minor, possesses exceptional chromatic power. These polychrome fragments painted on the boards of the 15th century choir stall undoubtedly deserve our fullest attention, and invite our reflection on the judgement they received in their day; it was only incomprehension that saved them from destruction. The decorative work on the wall alongside the choir, with its incrustations of glazed plant stems and leaves and auxiliary elements, calls for a similar response.

The baldachine-chandelier, the most potent piece in the entire intervention, is in fact the model which Gaudí and Jujol had assembled. This asks to be appreciated from the door in the main facade. The framing of the image of the Virgin and the subtle suspension of this great chandelier are worthy of prolonged study.

The pulpit, which stands to the left of the altar, has been dismantled at the time of writing, and can only be seen in photographs. Nevertheless, the treatment adopted for the stairs up to the pulpit is of interest.

As far as the stained glass windows are concerned, let me quote an entry in the Episcopal Records of the See of Palma de Mallorca for the 21st of July, 1910: "The Churchwarden stated that, in order to let light into the Corpus Christi chapel, he had seen to it that various holes were opened in the windows on the Gospel side, followed by further openings in the form of small windows, and added the same could be done in the San Jerónimo and Corona chapels".

Biography

1852 Born in Reus, Tarragona, on the 25th of June. Son of Francesc Gaudí i Serra and Antònia Cornet i Bertran.

1863 to 1868 Attends the Colegio de los Padres Escolapios in Reus.

1868 to 1873 Studies at the Escuela Provincial de Arquitectura in Barcelona.

1875 to 1877 Works in the studio of the architect Francesc de Paula del Villar i Lozano.

1876 Works alongside Josep Serramalera on various projects and as a draughtsman for the industrial machinery manufacturers Padrós i Borrás.

1877 to 1882 Works in collaboration with the master builder Josep Fontseré.

1878 Is awarded the professional qualification as an architect (March 5th). Descriptive memorandum on the project for the laying out of squares and promenades in the city of Barcelona (June). Manuscript on Ornamentation (August 10th). Makes the acquaintance of Don Eusebi Güell, his future patron and sponsor.
Wins a municipal competition with the sketch design of the streetlamps which now stand in the Plaça Reial in Barcelona. Over the next ten years Gaudí takes part in the trips organised by the Association of Architects of Catalonia and the "Associació Catalanista d'Excursions Científiques", the latter association being nationalist in character, with an interest in the study of Catalan antiquities and architecture. In 1883 he gets to know the work which Viollet-le-Duc carried out in the walled precinct of Carcassone in 1849.

1881 Takes part in the competition for the construction of a sailing club in San Sebastián, without winning any of the prizes. On the 2nd and 4th of February, *La Renaixença* publishes his article on the "Exposición de las Artes Decorativas" in the Institut del Foment del Treball in Barcelon. The general site plan of the Cooperativa Obrera Mataronense, which incorporates his first ideas, is published.

1882 Assists Joan Martorell in the controversial project for the facade of Barcelona Cathedral. Don Eusebil Güell purchases an elevation drawing of the Martorell project, lettered by Lluis Domènech i Montaner and drawn by Gaudí, subsequently reproduced in *La Renaixença* in February 1887. This drawing is now preserved in the "Arxiu Històric" of the Col·legi d'Arquitectes de Catalunya.

1883 On the recommendation of Joan Martorell, Gaudí is appointed to take over from Francesc de Paula del Villar i Lozano as architect in charge of the Expiatory Temple of the Sagrada Familia in Barcelona.

1887 Travels in Andalucía and Morocco in company with the 2nd marqués of Comillas.

1904 The Casa Calvet receives the first of the prizes awarded by the City Council, the Ajuntament of Barcelona, for the best building in the city.

1906 Takes up residence in the house designed by Berenguer in the Park Güell, although the last years of his life are to be spent entirely in his studio-cum-living quarters beside the Temple of the Sagrada Familia.

1908 Gaudí is asked to carry out a study for a hotel in New York City, of which a sketch by Joan Matamala has survived to the present day.

1910 Exhibition devoted to Gaudí's work in the Societé Nacional de Beaux Arts in Paris. This is to be the only exhibition of Gaudí's work held outside Spain during the architect's lifetime. As a result of his grave illness Gaudí is obliged to retire from public life. The following year, accompanied by his physician Don Pedro Santaló, he moves to Puigcerdà, Girona.

1914 Death of Francesc Berenguer Mestres, the architect and close friend of Gaudí's. From this time on, Gaudí's sole concern is with continuing his work on the Expiatory Temple of the Sagrada Familia.

1918 Death of Don Eusebi Güell (August 8th).

1922 For the first time an official body, the Congreso de Arquitectos de España, elects to pay homage to Gaudí's work.

1926 Gaudí is knocked down by a tramcar on the corner of the Gran Via de les Corts Catalanes and carrer Bailén, in Barcelona (June 7th). Three days later he dies, in the Hospital de la Santa Cruz, and is buried in the crypt of the Expiatory Temple of the Sagrada Familia.

Drawings by J. Renart. From left to right: Gaudí on March 6th, 1925; the architect *en son llit de mort*, June 1th, 1926, and Antoni Gaudí on May 8th, 1926

Chronology of projects and built work

1867 First drawings for the Reus magazine *"El Arlequín"*.

1867-1870 In collaboration with Josep Ribera and Eduard Toda, he works out a scheme for the restoration of the monastery of Poblet (Tarragona). His project report, the *Memoria de la Restauración del Monasterio de Poblet*, should not be overlooked.

1875-1876 Project for the Spanish Pavilion for the Philadelphia Centenary Exposition.

1876 Student project: Courtyard for the Diputación Provincial. Project for an academic competition: a pier.

1877 Project for a monumental fountain for the Plaça de Catalunya in Barcelona. Project for a General Hospital for Barcelona. Final project: a main hall for a university.

1877-1882 Collaborates with Josep Fontseré, master builder, on the project for the Parc de la Ciutadella.

1878 Scheme for streetlamps for the Plaça Reial (inaugurated in September 1879). Sketch design for the Casa Vicens. Glass display case to show gloves by Esteban Comella, for the Universal Exposition in Paris.

1878-1882 Project for the Cooperativa Textil Obrera Mataronense in Mataró. Design for a kiosk for Don Enrique Girosi.

1879 Decor for the Gibert pharmacy at no. 4, Passeig de Gràcia, in Barcelona (demolished in 1895).

1880 Scheme for the electric lighting of the Muralla de Mar, in collaboration with Josep Serramalera.

1882 Project for a hunting pavilion for Don Eusebi Güell in Garraf, Barcelona.

1883 Altar design for the chapel of Santo Sacramento in the parish church of Alella, Barcelona.

1883-1888 House for the tile manufacturer Don Manuel Vicens in carrer Sant Gervasi, now carrer de Les Carolines, 24-26. In 1925-1926, the architect Joan Baptista Serra Martínez widens a corridor of the house, and the walls and the boundary of the plot are changed. Gaudí is notified of the conversion.

1883-1885 House for Don Máximo Díaz de Quijano, "El Capricho", in Comillas, Santander. Site supervision of the project under construction is carried out by Cristóbal Cascante, a former fellow-student of Gaud'i's.

1884-1887 Pavilions on the Güell estate: gatehouse and stables on the Avinguda de Pedralbes in Barcelona, now home to the Cátedra Gaudí (inaugurated in 1953) of the Escola Técnica Superior de Arquitectura de Barcelona.

1884-1926 Expiatory Temple of the Sagrada Familia.

1886-1889 Palau Güell, a townhouse for Don Eusebi Güell and his family at no. 3-5, Carrer Nou de la Rambla. Since 1954 this building has housed the Barcelona Theatre Museum.

1887 Design for a pavilion for the Compañía Transatlántica for the Exposición Naval in Cádiz.

1887-1894 Episcopal Palace in Astorga, León. The commission comes from the bishop in person, a Reus man, the Ilmo. Sr. Don Joan Baptista Grau i Vallespinós. In September 1893, on the bishop's death, Gaudí resigns his post as supervising architect. In 1894 the diocesan architect of León, Blanch y Pons, is proposed as his successor. Starts work on the Palacio Manuel Hernández y Álvarez Reyero in 1899. In 1914 construction of the exterior of the Palace is completed under the direction of the architect Ricardo Guereta. In 1936 the building is used as a military headquarters, offices for the Falange and temporary quarters for artillerymen. In 1960, the bishop, Dr. Castelltor, starts on the definitive installation of the episcopal see in the Palace, although his sudden death prevents the completion of this work. His sucessor, the bishop Dr. González Martín, gives the building a new role, housing the Museo de los Caminos, which it still has today.

1888-1890 Theresan College at no. 41, carrer Ganduxer, Barcelona, to a commission by Don Enrique de Ossó, the Order's founder.

1891 Casa Fernández Andrés –"Los Botines"– in the Plaza de San Marcelo in León. Gaudí receives the commission from Don José y Aquilino Fernández Riu and Mariano Andrés Luna, acquaintances of Don Eusebi Güell.

The workroom in the office pavilion of the Temple of the Sagrada Familia in 1926. Gaudí at work in his studio in the Temple of the Sagrada Familia, drawn by R. Opisso

1892-1893 Scheme for a building for the Spanish Franciscan Missions in Tangiers.

1898-1904 Casa Calvet, at no. 48, carrer Caspe, Barcelona. Although the building bears the date 1899, the work of decoration, including the well-known furniture, made by Casas and Bardés, is not completed until 1904.

1898-1915 Crypt for the Colonia Textil Güell, in Santa Coloma de Cervelló, Barcelona. Although the work is started in 1908, it does not begin in earnest until 1912. The act of consecration is celebrated on the 3rd of Nov., 1915. Work on site is supervised by Gaudí's friend and assistant Francesc Berenguer.

1900-1902 Casa "Bellesguard", for Don Jaume Figueras, at no. 16-20, carrer Bellesguard, Barcelona. Joan Rubió i Bellver collaborates on the direction of work on site. In order to save the ruins of what was once the palace of King Martí l'Humà, Gaudí constructs a viaduct in 1908.

1900-1914 Park Güell, on the Muntanya Pelada, for Don Eusebi Güell, with the collaboration of Josep Maria Jujol.

1901-1902 Wall and gate for the estate of Don Hermenegild Miralles, in the Passeig de Manuel Girona.

1901-1902 Refurbishment of the marqués de Castelldosrius' house, now carrer Nova Junta de Commerç, Barcelona.

1902 At the request of Don Ricard Company, contributes to the decoration of the (no longer extant) Café Torino, at no. 18, Passeig de Gràcia, Barcelona, alongside Pere Falqués, Lluís Domènech i Montaner and Josep Puig i Cadafalch.

1903-1914 Restoration of the Cathedral of Ciutat de Mallorca, commissioned by the bishop, Pere Campins. Francesc Berenguer, Joan Rubió i Bellver and Jujol also participate.

1904 Scheme for a house for Don Lluís Graner.

1904-1906 Conversion to the Casa Batlló, at no. 43, Passeig de Gràcia, Barcelona, for Don José Batlló y Casanovas. Josep Maria Jujol also contributes to the scheme.

1906-1910 Casa Milà, "La Pedrera", at no. 92, Passeig de Gràcia, Barcelona, for Doña Rosario Segimon de Milà. Josep Maria Jujol participates in the project. In 1954, Francisco Javier Barba Corsini converts the attic into studio-apartments, adding a number of elements to the terrace.

1909-1910 Schoolrooms for the Expiatory Temple of the Sagrada Familia.

1912 Pulpits for the parish church in Blanes, Girona.

1923 Studies for the chapel of the Colonia Calvet in Torelló, Barcelona.

1924 Pulpit for a church in Valencia.

Bibliography

The bibliography on Antoni Gaudí is exceptionally extensive. The first important bibliography appeared in J. F. Ràfols Fontanals and Francesc Folguera's *Gaudí*, Editorial Canosa, Barcelona, 1929. This gives a comprehensive catalogue of books and articles published up to that date. *Antoni Gaudí and the Catalan Movement, 1870-1930*, by George R. Collins, with the support of the American Association of Bibliographers, was published in 1973 by the University Press of Virginia. The bibliography covers the complete range of publications on Gaudí and Catalan *Modernisme* up to 1970, approximately.

There has been no lessening of interest in the work of Gaudí since the latter volume appeared. I would, nevertheless, like to mention here a list of titles which I feel to be of essential importance:

Bassegoda Nonell, Juan, *Antoni Gaudí i Cornet*, Edicions Nou Art Thor, Barcelona, 1978.

Bassegoda Nonell, Juan, *Guía de Gaudí*, Edicions Nou Art Thor, Barcelona, 1988.

Codinachs, Macià (ed.), *Artículos manuscritos, conversaciones y dibujos de Antonio Gaudí*, Colegio Oficial de Aparejadores, Murcia, 1982.

Dalisi, Riccardo, *Gaudí, mobili e oggetti*, Electa Editrice, Milan, 1979.

Flores, Carlos, *Gaudí, Jujol y el Modernismo catalán*, Aguilar, S.A. de Ediciones, Madrid, 1982.

Hitchcock, Henry-Russel, *Gaudí*, Exhibition catalogue, MOMA, New York, 1957.

Le Corbusier, J. Gomis and J. Prats, *Gaudí*, Editorial RM, Barcelona, 1958.

Martinelli, César, *Gaudí. Su vida, su teoría, su obra*, Colegio de Arquitectos de Cataluña y Baleares, Comisión de Cultura, Barcelona, 1967.

Pane, Roberto, *Antonio Gaudí*, Edizione di Comunità, Milan, 1982.

Quetglas, José, "A. Gaudí i J. M. Jujol a la Seu", in *D'A*, Col·legi Oficial d'Arquitectes de Balears, Palma de Mallorca, winter 1989, pp. 40-71.

Sert, Josep Lluís and James Johnson Sweeney, *Antoni Gaudí*, Ediciones Infinito, Buenos Aires, 1969.

Solà-Morales, Ignasi de, *Gaudí*, Ediciones Polígrafa, Barcelona, 1983.

Solà-Morales, Ignasi de, *Eclecticismo y vanguardia. El caso de la Arquitectura Moderna en Catalunya*, Editorial Gustavo Gili, S.A., Barcelona, 1980.

Technische Hogeschool Delft, *Gaudí Rationalism met perfecte materiaal beheersing*, Universitare Press, Delft, 1979.

Xavier Güell, born in Barcelona in 1950, graduated in Architecture from the Escola Tècnica Superior d'Arquitectura de Barcelona, ETSAB, in 1977. With his own architect's office in Barcelona, he is actively involved with a number of specialised magazines and periodicals, as well as being the author of the books *Antoni Gaudí; Arata Isozaki. Barcelona Drawings*, and *Mediterranean Houses. Costa Brava*, and commissioning editor for the "Catlálogos de Arquitectura Contemporánea" collection, all of which are published by Editorial Gustavo Gili, S.A.